A Prospect of Cornwall

£8·00

By the same author

Cornish Villages
Cornish Hauntings and Happenings

A Prospect of CORNWALL

by

DONALD R. RAWE

ROBERT HALE · LONDON

First published in Great Britain 1986

Robert Hale Limited
Clerkenwell House
Clerkenwell Green
London EC1R 0HT

British Library Cataloguing in Publication Data
Rawe, Donald R.
A prospect of Cornwall. – (Prospect)
1. Cornwall – History
I. Title II. Series
942.3′7 DA670.C8

ISBN 0-7090-2585-8

Photoset in Plantin by
Rowland Phototypesetting Limited, Bury St Edmunds, Suffolk
Printed in Great Britain by St Edmundsbury Press Limited
Bury St Edmunds, Suffolk
and bound by Hunter & Foulis Limited

Contents

Illustrations		7
Preface		11
Introduction: Past and Present		13
Map		16
1	Prehistoric Cornwall	17
2	Rivers and Waterways	38
3	Market Towns and Boroughs	62
4	Fishing Ports and Harbours	79
5	Visitors' Cornwall	99
6	Traditions, Customs and Language	117
7	The Cornishman's Religion	132
8	The Cornishman's Work	154
9	Cottages, Farmhouses and Manors	175
10	Towards the 21st Century	204
Bibliography		213
Index		215

Illustrations by
James Lennon

Illustrations

Trevose, Dinas Head 18
Mulfra Quoit 20
Blind Fiddler, Trenuggo 23
The Hurlers stone circle on Bodmin Moor 25
Chysauster Iron Age village 29
Boleigh Fogou, St Buryan 32
Trethevy Quoit 34
St Piran's Cross, Penhale Sands, near Perranporth 36
Launceston: St Thomas Church and bridge over the Kensey 39
Horsebridge 40
Royal Albert Bridge, River Tamar, by Brunel 42
Newbridge over the Lynher 45
Golitha Falls, River Fowey 46
Restormel Castle 47
Lerryn Bridge 48
Treffry Viaduct, River Par 50
Restronguet Creek 52
Carrick Roads 54
Clapper Bridge on Bodmin Moor 55
Blisland 59
Rock village and quay 60
Hawker's Cove, Camel estuary 61
The South Gate, Launceston 63
Lostwithiel Bridge 65
Bodmin: Mount Folly Square and Law Courts 66
The bridge at Wadebridge 69
Truro 70, 71
Truro: Cathedral Square 73
Fore Street, Redruth 76
Coinagehall Street, Helston 78
Bude Canal 80
Port Isaac 81
Padstow: the inner harbour 83
Newquay Harbour 85

St Ives Harbour	86
A corner of St Ives	88
Custom House Quay, Falmouth	90
Charlestown	93
Fowey	95
Polperro	97
Botallack Tin Mine	100
The Cheesewring	102
Hayle	103
Gurnard's Head	105
Tintagel Castle	106
Newquay: view from the Bowling Club	107
The Fowey estuary: view from Polruan	108, 109
Padstow lifeboat being launched at Trevose Head	112
Treglos Hotel, Constantine Bay	113
Minack Theatre, Porthcurno	114
Wheal Martyn China Clay Museum	115
Hurling at St Columb Major	118
Padstow: May Day	120
Helston Furry Dance	121
Cornish wrestling	123
'Crying the Neck': about 1930	124
Gorseth Kernow: the Gorsedd of Cornwall	126
Scene from the *Ordinalia*, at Piran Round	128
Cross at Lanteglos (Camelford)	133
Celtic Cross, Lelant churchyard	134
Altarnun Church and Bridge	137
Mylor Church	138
Roche Rock	140
Octagonal spire of St Bartholomew's Church, Lostwithiel	142
St Just in Roseland	143
St Merryn Church	145
Come to Good Quaker meeting house, Feock	146
Centenary Wesleyan Church, Camborne	148
Wesley Memorial Chapel, Gwennap Pit	150
St Austell Church	151
Memorial to Billy Bray, Baldhu churchyard	152
Bosigran engine house	156
Wheal Coates engine house, St Agnes	158
Tin miners at work underground, about 1890	160
China clay workers, about 1920	163
2,000 feet below ground: the modern pumping station at South Crofty Mine	165
Calstock Viaduct	169

RNLI station, Whitesand Bay, Sennen 171
Steam train at Padstow station, about 1920 173
Moorswater Industrial Estate, Liskeard 174
An eighteenth-century farm labourer's cottage:
Roaring Stiles, St Keverne 177
Stone cottages at Crugmeer near Padstow 178
Slate cottages at Boscastle 180
Trevollard, St Veep 183
Cotehele House (the dining room) 184
Trerice House 186
Lanhydrock House (the Long Gallery) 188
Boconnoc House 191
St Michael's Mount 192
Trelissick House 194
Tregothnan House 195
Abbey House, Padstow 198
Launceston: town and castle 200
Walsingham Place, Truro 202
Godrevy Lighthouse and Point 205
Blackpool China Clay Drying Plant 207
Early warning system: Cleeve Camp, Morwenstow 209
Goonhilly Earth Satellite Station 210

To the memory
of my mother

Preface

All histories and topographies are necessarily selective, and this book may be thought to be more selective than most. Many and varied methods have been adopted to present surveys and histories of Cornwall over the last five centuries; I have been chiefly inspired by the invaluable works of John Norden and Richard Carew, both acutely perceptive commentators and reflectors of life in the Duchy. Believing profoundly in the continuing value of the historical dimension in our life today, I have selected areas of our past which seem to me to be the most relevant to our present awareness and needs.

Carew showed that a native Cornishman can evaluate his own land better than others may; if I have castigated or questioned many features of Cornwall, past and present, it has been in the hope that a more critical view will benefit us all in the future. Indeed, I would say that, if we do not all become much more vigilant over what is allowed to go on within our borders, we shall soon lose most of what we value in Cornwall and Cornish life today.

I must admit, without any apology, to being a devotee of the writings of Sir John Betjeman, to whom we should all be grateful; in his books and broadcasts over the years he has shown us how to look at our heritage in a fresh way, and especially to value its Victorian and Edwardian aspects.

I am also deeply indebted to the works of Canon L. E. Elliott-Binns, Dr A. L. Rowse, Charles Henderson, Dr A. K. Hamilton-Jenkin, Canon Miles Brown, Sir Nikolaus Pevsner, Dr John Rowe and so many others. The *History of Cornwall* by F. E. Halliday still stands as the best general book of its kind, though since its second edition of 1975 numerous developments, many of which I have tried to outline, have occurred.

Mr Craig Weatherhill has been most generous with advice and comment on Chapter 1, and Dr John Rowe on Chapter 8; my especial thanks are due to them both. I am also much indebted to Cornwall Fishermen Ltd, English China Clays Lovering Pochin Ltd, the Cornwall Chamber of Mines, the Industrial Development Department of Cornwall County Council, and the staff of the Royal Institution of Cornwall, Truro, who have readily answered many queries and provided information. Finally, I am most grateful to Mr Howard Inchbold for his help in compiling the index.

D.R.R.

Introduction
Past and Present

Many writers have tried to describe the magic of Cornwall – whatever is popularly supposed to be the essence or abiding spirit of the land, which draws people back to it year after year whether they be native-born or newcomers. That there is such a compelling attraction is undeniable; but its constituents are so varied, obscure and interfused that definition seems an impossibility.

One hopes of course that the fascination will endure, yet it is clear to many of us today that it is under acute threat from many directions. This book may well be regarded as yet another conservationist tract, for it seeks to record much that all lovers of Cornwall value and would protect: it attempts to revalue the past, to assess the rich heritage it has given us and to point out some ways in which it can be projected into the future.

But if there is one thing above all to be learned from any study of history it is, surely, that men and women, their interests and beliefs, are forever changing; that nothing stands still; that total preservation can never be achieved. The most enduring of our ancient monuments, such as the quoits and menhirs and stone circles, have always been under threat – as Chapter I will show, too many of them have been desecrated or destroyed down the centuries. Those that have survived suffer the depredations of wind and weather, and short of housing them in centrally-heated space-age domes they are bound to deteriorate, however slow the process may seem to us. Old buildings preserved by our generation are usually devoted to new uses undreamed of by their architects: chapels used as shops or flats; warehouses converted to restaurants or pubs; fish-cellars now become holiday cottages. It is a strange sort of preservation, yet in most cases the outer shell of those edifices – their traditional forms – thereby survive, and add their quota to the magic we all look for.

The Cornish miner of today, working with the latest drilling equipment under strict safety regulations and with the most modern processes of treating the ore he raises, may know or care little of the heroic and terrible lives of his predecessors in the eighteenth and nineteenth centuries. The modern fisherman with his radar and beam trawls, commanding a very reasonable price for the produce he lands, has in all likelihood forgotten the starvation endured by his ancestors in bad seasons, and the miserable return they received for their labour even in good ones. The Cornish farmer with all his expensive machinery, his silos and Dutch barns, Land Rovers and tractors, little considers the struggles of previous yeomen and tenants of his land to sweeten the soil and make it yield bare sustenance crops for the local populace. But we should all take account of these things, for out of the battles fought by our forebears against the elements and economic forces beyond their control has come, in our time, a land hugely worth living in, in which natural splendours are at last (despite the high unemployment rate) juxtaposed with an acceptable standard of living for the first time in recorded history.

The mementoes those previous generations have left us, their letters, accounts, wills and diaries, their buildings, hedges, monuments and implements, their attitudes and beliefs in religion, social usages and political ideals, their language, customs and festivities, their songs and poetry and prose, their drawings, pictures and photographs, have all, down to the poorest fashioned and most clumsily expressed, a real value to us today. Too many times has one generation turned on the things treasured by its immediate predecessor and thrown out onto the rubbish heap or burned in bonfires so much that the historian and antiquarian would have valued. Another all-important teaching of history is that we must not do the same, lest our children and their children revile us.

Thus the magic of Cornwall will go on working if we can only guard it well: not only 'treasure up the fragments that are left that nothing be lost' (*cuntelleugh an brewyon üs gesys na vo kellys travyth*) according to the motto of the Old Cornwall Societies, but actively breathe life into them by reliving their significance, and reinterpreting them for our present needs – for, as already remarked, nothing can ever be exactly the same again. The most outstanding example of revival in Cornwall today is the resuscitation of the Cornish language. It is not precisely the same tongue in all respects that our ancestors spoke in the past, though in its present form it does compare closely with the language at the height of its flowering, when the great Mystery Plays of the fourteenth and fifteenth centuries were performed. (We might consider that had Cornish continued to be handed down it would inevitably have changed, as Welsh and Breton have changed, and English today is changing, under the pressures of modern usage.) But today the language lives and breathes again, jealously guarded and passionately promoted by an ever-growing band of speakers and writers.

When every ancient monument, hill-fort and cliff-castle, medieval building and mining engine-house is protected by zealous groups of local people; when every dialect word and phrase, old saying and story, every song and dance and piece of music known to us (remember what a heritage was lost after the anglicization of Cornwall) has been written down, published, tape-recorded or filmed; when every feature of our complex past and manifold present is stored – if only in the memory of some great computer – then, only then, will those of us who are devoted to enjoying and extending the magic of Cornwall be able to rest.

Of course that day will never come. But if the next generation will value what we in our time have conserved, and will do better, the magic will continue to attract, enfold and delight the people of this land.

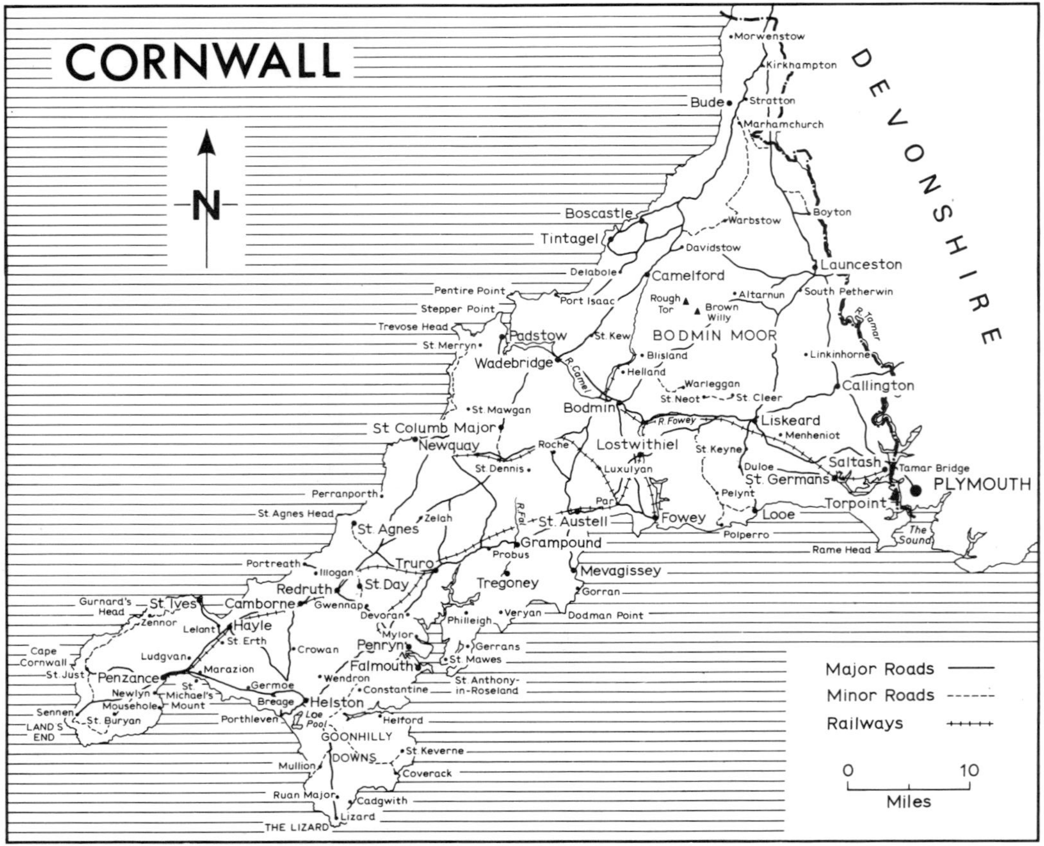

Based upon the Ordnance Survey map with the permission of the Controller of Her Majesty's Stationery Office. Crown Copyright Reserved.

I Prehistoric Cornwall

The view of Trevose Head is always magnificent, whatever the weather or time of year. Ten thousand years ago, however, it was very different. Instead of the grand curve of sand and rocks along Booby's and Constantine Bays, with their incessantly thundering breakers, and the little turf-covered peninsula of Constantine 'Island' jutting out between them, the hunters of the mesolithic or Middle Stone Age (about 8000 to 5000 BC) beheld a wide shelf of country stretching seaward below them, forested with birches, pines, oak, hazels and other trees.

The rocky islets we now call the Quies, Gulland, Newland and the Mouls appeared then as hills; they and the steep cliffs of Trevose itself rose up from a dense growth of bushes and trees. To the east, Stepper and Pentire Points also appeared as promontory heaths, with forested land between them; and the River Camel, much narrower than it is today, flowed out to sea between deep woods.

Although paleolithic (Old Stone Age) people roamed Cornwall and the south-west of Britain, they left little trace behind them. The first real evidence of community life comes from the Mesolithic Age, and the people of that time had a very different environment to contend with.

During the Ice Ages the sea level had, for some thousands of years, considerably fallen, and although afterwards as the ice packs shrank back towards the North Pole the sea rose again, there was still a remarkable difference between the coastline of the Middle Stone Age and ours today.

Mesolithic man was primarily a hunter pursuing wild boar, oxen, elk and aurochs; he devised weapons and tools to kill and dismember his prey, and these artefacts – flint axeheads, saws, scrapers and daggers – are still found today on Trevose Head, Constantine 'Island', Stepper Point, Bodmin Moor and Goonhilly Downs. The mesolithic families also gathered berries, fruits, nuts and edible fungi, and they were great fishermen. The coastal forests where they lived and hunted are now under the sea, detectable only by the sight of roots and branches rising from sand or mud at very low tides: at places such as Mount's Bay (St Michael's Mount was known, even in later Celtic times, as *Carrek Luz en Couze* – the Hoar Rock in the Wood), Perranporth, Maenporth and Bar Pool, Falmouth, Widemouth Bay and Maer Lake near Bude, Gillan, Portmellon, Mawgan Porth and several others. Other mesolithic forests lie under the alluvial soil which has since accumulated in the rivers and marshes at Hayle, Marazion, the Luxulyan Valley and Little Petherick in north Cornwall.

What has led some archaeologists to postulate that Middle Stone Age men were able to voyage long distances over the seas is the similarity of the rock chambers known as entrance graves found up and down the coasts of Scotland, Ireland, Cornwall, Scilly and the Channel Islands. Fish bones have been found in them, dateable to this epoch, and these fishermen may have been pursuing seasonal shoals of hake, bass, conger, ling and plaice in their hide-covered wickerwork boats. But the name 'entrance grave' may be a mis-

Trevose, Dinas Head

nomer: though human bones have been found in them, no complete skeleton has yet been found, and it may be that these were temples or depositories of votive offerings; perhaps the single member of a chief would be buried within as a cult object.

The best preserved of these chambers is Bant's Carn on St Mary's, Isles of Scilly; it is remarkably similar to one at Tramore, in south-east Ireland. Like most of them, it is set in a hillside and made of huge granite slabs, with an entrance passage leading to an inner chamber. Probably, as with so many primitive tribes all over the world, ancestor worship dominated their religious ideas.

About 3000 BC neolithic farmers sailed over to Cornwall from Spain or Brittany, and the New Stone Age began – though it is important to realize that the division of time into Ages is a very arbitrary scheme, that the newcomers did not displace their predecessors, and probably later mingled and married with them. The new arrivals are credited with the erection of the quoits or dolmens, so outstanding a feature of the Cornish landscape. How many of these great megalithic constructions there were originally is impossible to estimate: so much has been destroyed by later farmers and miners in their search for building and hedging stone. We are now left with thirteen, a concentration still far exceeding that found anywhere else in the British Isles. Seven of them are in West Penwith, on the moorland near Land's End; the others are scattered across west and north Cornwall and Bodmin Moor. Each consists of a huge granite capstone set on several upright stones weighing several tons; how they were put together without the aid of lifting-machines is still a matter of conjecture. The best preserved is Trethevy Quoit near St Cleer; Lanyon Quoit in Penwith and Pendarves near Camborne have been reconstructed; Pawton, near Wadebridge, has the largest capstone. Trebyan near Bodmin and the Devil's Quoit near St Columb are ruined and dispersed, though elements of them can be identified. These megaliths are known among Cornish archaeologists as Penwith-type chamber tombs (elsewhere, especially in Wales and Ireland, as portal dolmens). Each was probably heaped with soil originally, though the capstones would have been left bare to mark them. Since cremated remains have been found in them, the term tomb may well seem appropriate, but here again some reservation should be made; they may have been, like the entrance graves, centres of religious devotion, and the buried remains votive offerings to whatever deities were held to preside over the crops and herds of these people.

They were small, slender, dark-haired and long-headed. They had axes, primitive ploughs, deer-horn picks and stone hoes, and they began the age-long process of clearing the forest of hazel, juniper, oak, elm and birch from the valley sides and lower hillsides. They would clear sufficient land to create small fields in which to grow wheat, spelt and barley, moving on as they exhausted the fertility of the soil. Some of their field systems have been discovered at Carn Brea, Redruth, and others on Bodmin Moor and the West Penwith uplands.

Mulfra Quoit, West Penwith

Carn Brea was excavated under Thurstan Peter in 1911 and, much more thoroughly, under Dr Roger Mercer in 1970–3. This great hill, dominating the western part of Cornwall, was evidently an ideal site for these farmers and hunters to settle, above thick woods where animals roamed. Beneath the Iron Age fort discovered by Peter, Mercer and his associates unearthed the neolithic settlement, composed of a number of timber lean-to huts within a low stone wall, and beyond this the fields, cleared of boulders which had been made into cairns. Some nine hundred stone leaf-shaped arrowheads were found, and much pottery; some of these can be seen today in Truro Museum. A large granite saddle quern, or hand-mill for grinding corn, was another exciting find. The hunters covered a fair area of

Cornwall, as is evident from finds of axeheads and scrapers made throughout the parishes of Camborne and Redruth; other settlements must have existed nearby. Carn Brea itself supported about 150 people, which would indicate some five hundred in all over the district.

These New Stone Age people traded with others further east, exchanging greenstone axe and arrow heads from their own 'factories' around West Penwith and on east Bodmin Moor for flint artefacts from Dorset or Wiltshire. They also left us the first pottery remains, round-based ware with lugs for lifting, which they used for food storage and possibly also for cooking.

The Neolithic Age is generally believed to have been the era of construction of the great henge monuments of Britain, the best known being Avebury and Stonehenge. In Cornwall are to be found three lesser henges, consisting of circular earthen banks with ditches inside them, containing arrangements of standing stones. These are the Stripple Stones on Hawk's Tor near Blisland, Castilly Henge near Lanivet, and Castlewich near Callington. Eighteenth-century archaeologists like William Borlase mistakenly attributed them to the Druids of Celtic Britain; but although they may well have been used by the Druids for their rites, they certainly pre-date the arrival of the Druids by two thousand years or more. Arguments still run as to their original purposes; but, as at Stonehenge, all appear to have had a heel or altar stone on their western sides, upon which the rising sun would shine at certain equinoxes. It is not too fanciful to imagine human and other sacrifices taking place and, however barbaric the ceremonies, these seem to have been the churches and cathedrals of their age.

Around 2500 BC the Beaker people, vigorous, round-headed newcomers, arrived in Britain, bringing with them the techniques of smelting and working metal; in Cornwall they found tin and copper, which, fused together, produced a stronger and more resilient alloy promising far greater use. Thus began the Bronze Age, one of the greatest civilizing epochs of our history. The epithet 'Beaker' derives from these people's practice of burying their dead chieftains with various implements and also, invariably, a small bell-shaped or long-necked beaker, usually holding his ashes. Most of the burials were within tumuli or barrows; Cornwall has hundreds of these, easily detected humping against the skyline on the uplands, although untold numbers have been ploughed over and destroyed in the course of subsequent history.

Bronze Age people are also credited with the erection of stone circles and alignments of menhirs (*maen*, stone; *hyr*, long) in which Cornwall is so rich. Although they are found all over Britain and on the Continent (especially in Brittany), only the Wiltshire Downs has a comparable concentration of them. There are groups of them on Bodmin Moor, including the Trippet Stones, the Leaze Circle below Garrow Tor, the Fernacre Circle and Stannon Stones below Roughtor, and three circles near the Hurlers (St Cleer). There is the Nine Maidens alignment on St Breoke Downs, and in West Penwith the Merry Maidens at Rosmodress, Boscawen Un circle (later used by the Celts as a site for their Bardic Gorseths) and other circles at Tregaseal, Boskednan and Treen Common in Zennor – though it is argued that this latter may be a neolithic henge. There are two circles in Wendron parish, and others, in debased forms due to later removals of stones, at Leskernick and Goodaver in Altarnun, three in St Breward parish, and one on Craddock Moor, St Cleer. All these are of granite; at Duloe in south-east Cornwall is a quartz circle. The stones range from about two feet to six feet in height above the ground.

Discounting the popular tale of girls being changed into stones for dancing on Sunday, it used to be thought that the name Nine Maidens, which is attached to a number of stone circles, was derived from *medn*, a late Cornish form of *meyn*, stones, and *naw*, Cornish for nine, or *nawnjek*, nineteen. It may be so, but these names probably date back only to the eighteenth or nineteenth century; recent plottings of the stones and of impressions of those removed reveal that most circles originally had more than twenty monoliths, a few (like Louden Hill) over thirty, and two (Fernacre and Stannon) a massive seventy to ninety.

A further Bronze Age feature is the number of single menhirs or standing stones, erected for some ceremonial or commemorative purpose. Most of them stand in lonely majesty among the heather and furze of the uplands; for example, the Blind Fiddler, eleven feet of quartz-studded granite on open downs at Trenuggo near Drift in West Penwith. Other remarkable longstones are found at Lelant (the Beersheba Stone), Boswen in Pendeen, Carfury in Madron, a pair (The Sisters) at Higher Drift, Kerrow in Zennor, Pridden in St Buryan (now leaning at an angle of forty-five degrees), Trelew in St Buryan, Try at New Mill, and Tresvenneck Drift. The largest extant monolith in Cornwall is the Men Gortos (Stone of Waiting) on St Breoke Downs near Wadebridge.

Along with the chamber tombs, dolmens, tumuli and stone circles, these have attracted the attention of archaeologists from the time of Dr Borlase, the father of Cornish archaeology, onwards. All the Bronze Age monuments seem to have strong connections with burial rites; bones and ashes have been found in either urns or kists made of slate or granite slabs, at many sites. The barrows certainly appear to

Blind Fiddler, Trenuggo

be graves, or at least the memorials, of single important persons; in them some of their bones or ashes were placed with other valuable artefacts – flints, glass, arrowheads or pottery. Unlike the mesolithics or neolithics with their entrance graves and dolmens, the Beaker Folk had evolved the idea of single monument or grave for each chief or great man, though, once buried, he would doubtless be accounted a god or paternal spirit and probably worshipped.

So the dead of the Bronze Age dominate west Cornwall and Bodmin Moor still, on areas of land that have escaped the ploughs of the last four thousand years. They were actually once commemorated all over Cornwall (in fact, all over Britain), mainly, it seems, on the uplands – for all those circles, barrows and standing stones command fine views; but so many have fallen victim to the needs of latter-day farmers, miners, builders and road-makers that we shall never know their full extent. The largest recorded menhir in Cornwall, the Maen Pern in Constantine near Falmouth, which stood twenty-four feet tall, was wantonly destroyed in the eighteenth century. Dr Borlase wrote that it 'made above twenty stone posts for gates, when it was clove up by the farmer'. Such monoliths were great temptations during the industrial age which followed, and the numerous engine-houses and other remains of tin- and copper-mines must contain stone from many of them.

Several Bronze Age settlements have been excavated on Bodmin Moor. In 1910 a St Ives antiquarian, R. J. Noall, failed to dissuade the farmer and stone-cleavers from destroying another settlement near his home. Such acts of unfeeling destruction are less common today but still occur. Normally nowadays the Cornwall Archaeological Society or the Cornwall Committee for Rescue Archaeology is able to examine the site before development occurs. In 1970–3 six barrows were excavated on Hensbarrow (north of St Austell) before they were buried by expanding china clay sand dumping.

Bodmin Moor is disappearing under the processes of ploughing and pasturing at the rate of ninety-five acres (fifteen square kilometres) each year, and the Penwith moors are under severer attack. The encouragement given by the European Community, in the form of bounties to hill farmers to 'reclaim' hillside land, is the main problem. (The farmers are actually cultivating what was never farmland, except for those tiny field systems which surely ought to be preserved.) One continually returns to the question, can we justify present-day commercial gains against the preservation of ancient remains and monuments? Many tumuli are known to us only through past records or in place-names. Up to the end of the eighteenth century the area around Holmbush, now part of St Austell, contained some twenty barrows, now lost under building developments. Near Padstow are two revealing names, Crugmeer (the Great Barrow) and Trig Troal (*crig toll*: the barrow on the hill brow); the tumuli have long been levelled by ploughing.

Perhaps the most enigmatic of Bronze Age relics are the holed stones, found mainly in West Penwith; the most famous are the Men an Tol (*men*, stone; *an tol*, of the hole) on the moors above Madron. Since medieval times there has been a prevailing belief that children would be safeguarded against rickets by passing them through the hole; perhaps this was a folk-memory, handed down from the Bronze Age. Originally the stone may have had a fertility significance, symbolizing the female sexual organ. Near the Men an Tol are two phallic longstones associated with it, though they have actually been moved during the last century or two to form an alignment with it. Another holed stone, now used as a gatepost, can be seen in the hedge opposite the entrance to Rosmodress circle. A series of six holed stones, much smaller, occurs on the south-east slopes of Carn

The Hurlers stone circle on Bodmin Moor

LENNOX

Kenidjack near St Just. A single stone, the Tolven, stands in a cottage garden at Constantine.

Sedentary agriculture was first practised during the Bronze Age (the neolithic peoples, having cleared a glade or hillside, would move on after obtaining a few crops from it); so the Beaker Folk must have discovered the means of fertilizing the land. Few ancient civilizations have left us such a mighty collection of artefacts and monuments as this one did. At its height, Professor Stuart Piggot deduced, there was an aristocratic Wessex culture dominating Britain, trading with the Baltic (for amber beads, among other things) and Mycenaean Crete, for gold and bronze ornaments, weapons and faience beads, which have been found on Salisbury Plain and elsewhere. These remote Britons could weave and wore clothes fastened with buttons and pins of bone and copper.

Their trading led to extensive links with the great Mediterranean civilizations, via overland France, and with Ireland, the main source of gold. Cornwall must have been important to them, especially to supply tin and copper, but apart from this trade there were few links with Wessex. Left to themselves, its few thousand farmers and hunters developed in their own way. They evidently traded the metal found on outcrops and in streams for Irish gold; witness the three magnificent lunulae found in the middle of the nineteenth century, two at Harlyn Bay, one at St Juliot (now in Truro Museum). These intricately wrought moon-shaped pieces were no doubt the insignia of office of their great men, worn round their necks on ceremonial occasions, and were found buried in kists where their ashes had also been interred.

A number of valuable Bronze Age finds have been made west of the Tamar and are to be inspected mainly at the Royal Institution of Cornwall, Truro: the Fowey Rapier, some two feet long, dredged up in the estuary there in 1980, is of the same period as the rapier mould of the same shape found at Bodwen, Lanlivery – about 1100–950 BC. There is also the Pelynt sword, a fragment only but which gives us a perfect idea of the whole; it strongly resembles swords found in graves at Mycenae. Dated around 1600–1500 BC, it is the only one of its kind so far known to have been imported into north-west Europe. A bronze sword-blade, found in the ground by a cattle-trough in 1952 at Carn Pessack, St Keverne, is similar to swords from the Thames valley, dating from 1000–800 BC. There are spearheads of bronze from the Middle Bronze Age, large bar-lug cooking-pots, battle-axes and bracelets; also necklets and torcs of gold from Ireland, from a hoard found at Amalveor, Towednack, near St Ives. All these present a picture of a people enterprising in trade, agriculture and warfare, who in adopting cremation instead of inhumation perhaps believed in purification and spiritual values previously unthought of.

It seems unbelievable that such an advanced people could not write (most contemporary Mediterranean and Near Eastern cultures had sophisticated scripts). Certainly nothing on their artefacts or memorials can be interpreted as writing. It is possible that they wrote on skins or parchment, which have not survived. By the late Bronze Age the upland and moorland sites were becoming much damper and colder; the soils were turning acid, with the spread of heather and gorse, as we know it today. The hazels and junipers and scrub oaks were declining. Human remains in graves dating from this time have been found badly or totally decayed; no skin material could have survived. In the later Bronze Age, therefore, there was considerable migration down to coastal or lowland sites such as Trevisker, and Gwithian near Hayle, where timber structures were built and where a good deal of pottery and other remains have been excavated. But, perhaps due to the ravages of later farming, perhaps to the comparatively short length of time a parchment or skin can survive in our moist climate, nothing from the Bronze Age has survived in writing.

Nor could the next wave of people to occupy Cornwall (and Britain) write, at least in their early stages. But because Roman and other authors have given us accounts of them, we do know much more about them. They were the Celts, a warlike but highly advanced race, the first tribes of whom arrived from Continental Gaul and Belgium around 500 BC and swept through to Ireland. The second group arrived a century or so later and settled all over mainland Britain: they were the Brythonic tribes, whose name the land bears, and in their way they left as great an impress on the Cornish landscape as their predecessors. They possessed the technique of working a metal more accessible and useful, though less precious, than bronze; thus the Iron Age was ushered in.

The Celtic civilization at its height stretched from the Danube to Spain, and to north Britain; its works are found all over that area, which has been called the Celtic Empire, though no single emperor ever ruled it. The Celts brought not only a new form of warfare but a new attitude to the past and the future: they were poets, musicians and dreamers, men of religion (though today we might be inclined to label much of it, too easily, as superstition) and intricate crafts, as well as doughty warriors.

They were also great shipbuilders and voyagers. The level of their decoration, as found on urns, cups, shields and torcs, reached heights undreamed of by previous peoples and hardly touched since. Their weaving was an advanced process and included tweeds; when Julius Caesar arrived in Britain in 55 BC, he found the British Celts dressed in brightly coloured 'chequered clothes' (including *bracchae*, breeches, which he had never seen before) – the ancestors of the modern tartans so splendidly displayed today not only by the Scots but also by the Celts of Wales, the Isle of Man and Cornwall.

From about 200 BC through to AD 100 a tremendous series of hill forts, rounds and cliff castles were thrown up all over Cornwall, Devon, Somerset, Wiltshire and Dorset – indeed, all over Britain, though Cornwall in particular has more of such constructions to the square mile than any other area. Each fort must have taken several months if not years to build, by digging out great trenches and banking up the earth and stone thus gained. Each needed a sizeable community to achieve it; even the smaller rounds would require a dozen or twenty men working for such extended periods: the largest, such as Castle an Dinas in St Columb parish, and Chûn Castle in West Penwith, needed perhaps fifty to a hundred. Some thirty hill forts have been identified within Cornwall, and twenty-two sites of cliff-castles, extant or decayed. Along with the thousands of other place-names bequeathed to us by the Brythonic Celts, J. B. Gover in his *Place Names of Cornwall* (in the library of the Royal Institution of Cornwall, Truro) lists over two hundred names containing the elements *car*, *din* or *dun*: terms denoting fortress or castle. Although some Iron Age hill-forts were evidently built on the sites of Bronze Age settlements, it does seem undeniable that a new wave of dominant settlers had come in to perpetrate all this. What or whom did they fear, that they should adopt such a policy of building massive works? That question has never been satisfactorily resolved.

No doubt they needed to defend their people and livestock from various enemies, mainly other Celtic tribes and, especially in Cornwall and Wales, from incursion by the raiding Gaels from Ireland. Two thousand years ago Cornwall must have been a patchwork scene of raiding and fighting Iron Age communities. However, theories are now being advanced that the hill-top forts were built at least partly for religious and social activities. The number of Iron Age rounds in Cornwall which are called either *plain-an-gwarry* (the place of the play) or Playing Place would certainly lend credence to this. There is Piran Round, above Perranporth; St Just Round, in the centre of that village in West Penwith; others at St Hilary, at Ruan Lanihorne, south of Truro, and at Castilly Henge; and others which have disappeared, being known only by name, such as Plain and Gwarry at Redruth and the former Playing Place at Padstow.

Soon after the period of building these forts, the Celts seem to have settled into a more peaceful existence and developed hundreds of *trefs* (farm homesteads) all over the country; although some castles and forts bear evidence of later re-occupation, it seems that these defence camps were used only intermittently, perhaps in time of danger, perhaps also for votive rites, councils and other gatherings. We may imagine the farming peoples of the districts around Caer Bran in west Cornwall, Castle an Dinas, dominating mid-Cornwall, and Castle Canyke, near Bodmin on the overland route from Ireland to Brittany, going up to each immense *dinas* with its earthen banks and ditches and central causeway leading into it, to celebrate their Celtic festivals.

The complex pattern of Iron Age settlement in Cornwall includes groupings of courtyard houses, each combining living-quarters, workshop, a stable and a store within one building. These are found exclusively in West Penwith. These beautiful houses of granite stones, arranged with their rooms around a central courtyard (their thatched or turfed roofs have, of course, long disappeared), are detectable at eleven sites in Penwith. The best examples, now excavated and open to the public by courtesy of the Department of

Chysauster Iron Age village

the Environment, are Chysauster near Penzance and Carn Euny near Sancreed. Some of them are eighty feet in length. More than two dozen others can be seen at Mulfra Vean and Cranken, New Mill: Bosullow and Crofto in Morvah; Goldherring, Sancreed (now much overgrown by gorse and heather); Bosporthennis and Porthmeor near Treen, overlooking Gurnard's Head; near Trevean Round in Morvah; and Boswarva in Madron. All existed amid intensively worked, small, square fields, minute by present-day standards. Such plots were worked by light ploughs without coulters to turn the earth and therefore had to be cross-ploughed to achieve successful seeding. Many of the fields now worked in West Penwith and some on Bodmin Moor are actually of Iron Age origin, some extending back to the Bronze Age, having been amalgamated by later removals of the bouldered hedges into larger squares. But the small historic fields show up clearly enough from aerial photographs.

The fogous (Cornish *ogo, fogo*, cave) of Cornwall are another fascinating mystery. There are eleven, all west of the Fal; many are ambitious constructions in granite blocks, comprising an underground passage with two entrances, and sometimes with chambers or rooms leading off it. They may have been used as underground or above-ground storage caves, Iron Age cool larders; they could also have been used as refuges for the village women and children in times of attack. Again, a figure drawn on the walls of Boleigh Fogou, St Buryan, seems to portray a god-figure, with spear in one hand and serpent in the other: does he represent Cernunnos, god of the Celtic Underworld, and were votive offerings made to him? Were fogous actually temples to the Dark Gods?

The most accessible fogou is that at Carn Euny Iron Age village, which is in the care of the Department of the Environment and open to the public. Haliggey Fogou, just outside the grounds of Trelowarren House near Helston, is also extremely well cared for and accessible. Pendeen Vau, just below the farmyard of the manor farm of Pendeen, can be examined with permission from the occupier, as can Boleigh (in the grounds of Rosmerrin House, St Buryan). Lower Boscaswell Fogou is accessible off a lane near the cliffs. The remains of other fogous can be seen at Chysauster and at Porthmeor near Gurnard's Head. There are also possible remains of them at Bosullow in Morvah, Crankan near New Mill, and Bosporthennis near Treen (north), all above ground; another above-ground fogou, Trevean Round in Morvah, was destroyed in 1913. There is an accessible fogou a mile north of Constantine village, near Helston, and one exists, or existed, somewhere in St Hilary parish; possibly it has been covered over. It is probable that all the fogous were originally associated with courtyard house settlements, some of which have disappeared.

An historic discovery, made in 1900, of 130 Iron Age graves in the sand at Harlyn Bay near Padstow, does not fit the general pattern of Iron Age remains, and reinforces the idea that the Celts did not massacre or drive out their predecessors. The small, dark, long-headed people whose skeletons were found in stone kists at Harlyn are neolithic rather than Celtic or Bronze Age types; to the taller, fairer Celts they must have seemed almost pygmies. The hypothesis that the folklore of Cornish piskies and giants comes from a juxtaposition of these two dissimilar races may well be a valid one. Other similar Iron Age cemeteries have been found, one at Trevone, a mile or two from Harlyn, and another at Trelan Bahow in the Lizard peninsula. (The Celts had cemeteries, but their dead, being buried in earth and probably in wooden coffins, have not been preserved.) Even today the Neolithic type can be seen in Cornwall: short, black-haired, heavily eyebrowed, often without lobes to their ears.

That the Romans came to Cornwall and garrisoned it over a period of perhaps three centuries or more is no longer in any doubt. Their contribution to the landscape was, it appears, only slight; they seem to have been interested primarily in the tin trade. (They had tin-mines in Spain but were no doubt seeking alternative supplies.) A square Roman fort exists at Tregear, Nanstallon, on the Camel valley slopes – on the overland route from Padstow to Fowey, one route for the export of Irish gold and Cornish tin to the Continent. Other camps above Helford river, near Gweek, another at Bosence near Hayle, may have been occupied by Roman garrisons; all are evidently associated with tin workings and routes.

Roman milestones, indicating routes and perhaps projected road-works, are found at Trethewy, Gwennap, Breage, Tintagel and St Hilary, and a Roman villa at the second century AD has been partly excavated at Magor, near Camborne, with a tessellated floor. It was probably the house of an official who retired there, maybe a native Celt who had taken service under Rome and who decided that his homeland was the place to spend his last years in. Most of these remains lie within tin-bearing areas. The Roman government system of roads was supplemented by tracks, the use of which also continued in the post-Roman period; there are several other tracks across Exmoor and north Devon. There is as yet no real evidence for an actual Roman road in Cornwall, but the alignment of the names Stratton, Longford and Forestreet in north Cornwall, taken with the character of the road joining those places with its wide verge, suggests one strong possibility. The names all contain the elements 'street' or *forth* (Cornish, road).

LENNON

Considerable Roman coin hoards have been found, at St Michael Caerhayes, Turnaware Point on the Fal estuary, Gear in Lamorran, Malpas, Lerryn, and near the Hayle Causeway, among other sites. A fine Roman altar in local granite is now in the gardens of Tresco, Scilly, where, badly weathered, it continues to deteriorate. It originally came from St Mary's, where evidence for a Romano-British settlement has been found.

In AD 410 the Romans left Britain to defend itself against the growing incursions of Germanic tribes. Soon afterwards Arthurian history and legend begin, for the balance of opinion is that a Roman-trained general named Arthur rallied the Britons around AD 490–517 and won twelve successive victories over the invaders. In Cornwall an historic conundrum presents itself. Later Welsh writings, including the story of Cwlhuch and Olwen, tell us that Arthur had a Court (more probably a camp or regional headquarters) at Kelliwic in Kernow. The place name Kelliwic existed, as we know from the Assize Rolls of 1302, which mention a Thomas de Kelliwic, murdered in Penwith. Kelliwic (the Place of the Grove) has been identified variously with Callington, with Callywith near Bodmin and with Castle Killibury, a hill-fort north of Wadebridge. Not far from Killibury is Slaughterbridge, by Camelford; a later tradition has grown that it was the site of Arthur's last battle against Mordred. But here we enter the world of myth and legend created by writers such as Geoffrey of Monmouth (who never came to Cornwall) and Sir Thomas Mallory, and the mists of romance envelop us.

A few likelihoods do, however, emerge for us to hold on to. Arthur, whether or not he was a king, was Pendragon or commander-in-chief, and though his main headquarters was probably at Cadbury-Camelot, an obvious fort from which to oppose the Saxon advances from the Thames Valley, he might well have had a camp in Cornwall and been born a Dumnonian – indeed a Cornishman, if there is anything in the story of how Uther fathered him on Igerna, wife of Gorlois, Duke of Cornwall.

Near Fowey, an inscribed menhir reminds us of another great legend, the love story of Tristan and Iseult. Although tradition places Mark's Court at Tintagel, if his palace were indeed in Cornwall (it may have been in Brittany), it would have been in the Fowey valley. Castle Dore, an Iron Age earthwork dominating the west bank and re-occupied by the Celts of the sixth century, is there; but so is Lantyan, its name corresponding to Lancien, Mark's palace in the oldest existing *Romance of Tristan* (written by Béroul in the twelfth century). 'Drustanus', a form of Tristan, recorded on the longstone

Boleigh Fogou, St Buryan

nearby, is the earliest known occurrence of the name. Recent scholarship concludes that the legend of Tristan and Iseult originated within Cornwall; even the name Iseult (given to a ford in Meneage, known as Hyrt Eselt) is found in Cornwall earlier than anywhere else.

Inscribed longstones commemorating tribal chieftains, heroes or kings are to be found along the western seaboards of both Britain and Ireland. With 145 known in Wales and twelve north of Hadrian's Wall, the fifty identified in Cornwall, Scilly, Lundy, Devon and Somerset (the area covered by Dumnonia) bespeak a continuing intercourse between the western Celts. This was, after all, the Age of the Saints, when holy men moved across the channels and seas perpetually seeking to proselytize their faith. Most of the stones are, in fact, associated with early Christian graveyards, which have continued in use as sites of worship and burial down the centuries; even those which survive in splendid isolation, like the Tristan Stone and the Men Scryfa on Madron Downs in Penwith, appear to have had crosses inscribed on them and presumably commemorate notables who became Christian.

The Rialobranus (Royal Raven) whose name is inscribed on the Men Scryfa (Stone of Writing) may have been of the local royal family who constructed or re-occupied Caer Bran fort a few miles away, although Bran (Cornish, a crow or raven) was a common enough name. But these enigmatic memorials will long challenge us to guess exactly who they commemorate; we are not likely to learn much more of Selus at St Just, Ulcagnus at Lewannick, Ignioc at St Clement, and so many others.

There is a small concentration of the inscribed stones north of the Camel estuary, at St Kew, St Endellion, Worthyvale and Tintagel. In addition to their Roman inscriptions most of these present the names of the dead cut along their edges in the strokes of the Ogam alphabet, developed in Ireland a century or so before they were erected; there is a large scatter of such stones all over south-west Ireland. It seems that the Irish incursions up the Camel have left these enduring marks; unless native Cornishmen, trading with the Irish, adopted Ogam themselves – an unlikely thesis. The practice of commemorating kings and heroes with such stones went on, here and there, until the eighth or ninth century. Near St Cleer is the ornately wrought Doniert Stone, widely held to be a memorial to Dungarth, King of Cornwall, drowned in the River Fowey in the year 871 or 875; and in the gardens of Penlee House, Penzance, is a magnificent eight-feet-tall cross inscribed *Regis Ricati Crux* – King Ricatus' Cross. Ricatus may have been the penultimate Cornish king; the cross can be dated

Trethevy Quoit

to between AD 900 and 930, and Ricatus' presumed successor, Howell or Hywal, submitted to Athelstan around AD 930.

Contemporary with many of these highly regarded stones – which are, of all our ancient monuments, one hopes, the least vulnerable to the depredations of modern vandalism – are the hundreds of Celtic crosses in their various forms erected up and down Cornwall, conspicuously reminding us of the Christian heritage of the sub-Roman and sadly misnamed Dark Ages. They are a great study in themselves, spanning some four or five centuries. Such works as Langdon's *Cornish Crosses* and Sir John Maclean's *History of Trigg Minor*, as well as those of Borlase and others, have recorded most of them for us, and the fieldwork of the Cornwall Archaeological Society and Old Cornwall Society members continues to keep their preservation in our minds. Such a heritage in a small country the size of Cornwall is unique, and these noble granite memorials with

St Piran's Cross, Penhale Sands, near Perranporth

wheel-heads, most of them with four holes or a carved crucifix, are to be found along the length and breadth of the Duchy: in churchyards, by the wayside, at crossroads – in fact, wherever Celtic missionaries and hermits chose to preach their own distinctive version of the faith then sweeping all over Europe.

2 Rivers and Waterways

For millions of years the rivers of Cornwall have scored and fretted their way through the landscape, profoundly altering it. They have highly individual characters and during the past have been great highways of trade and travel.

The Tamar, the longest, is also the noblest and most famous, being the traditional frontier of Cornwall. Its east bank was fixed as the boundary by Athelstan of Wessex after he had defeated the last Cornish king, and behind it the Cornish were, by and large, left alone – though increasingly, from the late tenth century on, parts of east and then mid and west Cornwall were infiltrated. The Normans built castles and manor houses (the Conqueror's half-brother, Robert of Mortain, became Earl of Cornwall) but did not mingle with the Cornish or Saxons. So the Cornish kept their own language for some six or seven centuries, though it gradually retreated in face of increasing commerce and involvement with English wars. But even today, as the CORNWALL-KERNOW signboards on the bridges announce, west of Tamar is another people, another little world.

Ptolemy (AD 120) mentions the Tamar in his *Geography*; its name shares a common Celtic root with other rivers such as the Tay, Taw and Torridge. Its main source is under Woolley Barrows by Kilkhampton, and the several streams join in heath country at Tamar Lakes. The first of these was constructed in 1819 to provide water for the Bude–Holsworthy Canal; the second, a water reservoir, was opened in 1967. Today boating and fishing there attract locals and holiday-makers alike.

After passing under its first bridge, Tamarstone, the young river reaches Bridgerule – named after Ruald Adobed, the Norman who held the manor of Brigge and who built the first bridge there. North Tamarton, six miles below, is the first real village: a sleepy place today, with memories of a fierce struggle on its bridge between Fairfax's troops and the Royalists, and of Robert Stephen Hawker (author of the Trelawny ballad), curate there from 1831 to 1834. Like another famous parson-poet, Robert Herrick, he kept a favourite pig, a Black Berkshire named Gyp who, well groomed and intelli-

Launceston: St Thomas Church and bridge over the Kensey

gent, would accompany him on parish visits. When Hawker's sister at nearby Whitstone objected to Gyp's entering her house, Robert retorted, 'He's as well behaved as any of your family.'

After flowing through rich agricultural land, the broadening Tamar reaches Boyton and Werrington. Until 1972 Werrington and North Petherwin parishes were part of Devon – a legacy of the first Saxon encroachment over the Tamar. Now the river along its length is the border. At Werrington are an endearing manorial church and an informal garden covering many acres, with a tasteful Victorian house set amid it. The Attery or Ottery, the first considerable tributary, comes in below Werrington; fourteenth-century Yeolmbridge, over it, is one of the oldest and best preserved of Cornish bridges.

Below this confluence more rivers come together: the Kensey, flowing in from the Cornish moors, and the Carey and Lyd from Dartmoor. Wider but still rapidly flowing, the Tamar now reaches Launceston, the town rising above its west bank. Here above the Gateway to Cornwall the Normans built their huge and commanding castle. Polson or Polston Bridge, where the main road used to cross, was rebuilt in the nineteenth century, but not happily: Charles Henderson (the Cornish historian) called it a piece of mid-Victorian vandalism. It has now been superseded by a modern road bridge

Horsebridge

carrying the dual carriageway, so that one hardly notices, at high speeds, the transition from Cornwall-Kernow to Devon; it is a brief hail and farewell, all over in the blink of an eyelid.

Launceston was the beginning of the Royal Cornish Way – for kings, earls and dukes of Cornwall entered via Polson. The Romans must have used the route before them, continuing down to Nanstallon (Tregear Fort), Bosence near Hayle and St Michael's Mount. In the Middle Ages this was part of the pilgrims' route from the West of England to Spain: they travelled via Palmer's Bridge over the upper Fowey, the hospice of Temple on the moor, Bodmin and Perranzabuloe (where saintly relics were to be viewed), down to Marazion, Mousehole or Penryn, there to take ship for Santiago de Compostella, the third shrine in Christendom. Today the A30 main road brings in and out the bulk of goods and travellers along practically the same route.

Through green and fertile farmland beyond Lawhitton, the Tamar reaches Greystone Bridge and some incomparable steep-sided wooded valleys. Greystone, named after the medieval manor, is early fifteenth century. That was a time of intense church rebuilding, and the construction and repair of bridges, held to be a Christian necessity, were widely encouraged; there was even a brotherhood of bridge-building friars who travelled about in this cause. Bishop Lacey of Exeter in 1439 granted an Indulgence of forty days to all who contributed funds to Greystone. (It actually meant forty days less in Purgatory for the donor.) This practice of issuing Indulgences may well be criticized today as being corrupt, but the results are still there for us to see in many a beautiful and sturdy old bridge. Greystone, 225 feet long with five great semicircular arches, over the placidly flowing trouty Tamar among centuries-old woods, is one of the noblest of its kind.

Winding below an Iron Age camp on Castlepark Hill and by Carthamartha hamlet (the name seems to contain the elements *caer*, camp or fort, and Margh or Mark – was King Mark ever here?), the Tamar receives the Inney, flowing in from Davidstow Moor where it rises nineteen miles away. It has chattered through somnolent St Clether and bosky Laneast, and past Polyphant quarry, supplier of so much fine stone for church rebuilding. Four miles further down, the Tamar valley widens to lush pastures on the Cornish side, as the river reaches Horsebridge.

This excellent edifice, Greystone's twin and surely built by the same unknown architect (probably employed by the abbot of the Benedictine monastery at Tavistock), was the subject of an Indulgence granted two years before that of Greystone. The name comes from the Norman–French *haute*, high (Haute Bridge, Leland,

1539). Until the building of New Bridge at Gunnislake, this was the main route from Tavistock to Launceston.

Wide meanders develop below Horsebridge, and the Tamar almost doubles back on itself between the villages of Luckett and Latchley. Now among conifer woods it reaches Newbridge and Gunnislake, where the high spring tides reach. Neither Gunnislake nor Calstock, four miles below, has yet completely recovered from the demise of their great days of mining tin and copper, though flower- and fruit-growing, quarrying and a steady tourist trade (mainly river trips from Plymouth) are slowly reviving them. Newbridge is said to have been begun by Sir Piers Edgcumbe of Cotehele House, just below Gunnislake, who died in 1539; it is finely proportioned of moorstone (free granite lying on the moors), twelve feet wide as it was originally built. Sir Piers no doubt considered Horsebridge rather too far to go when crossing into Devon. A sharp

Royal Albert Bridge, River Tamar, by Brunel

exchange on the bridge in 1644 resulted in the Royalists under Sir Richard Grenville losing two hundred men, taken prisoner by Essex's Roundheads.

Between steep pastures and orchards on the Cornish side, and the magnificent wooded bluff of Morwellham with the Morwell rocks on the Devon bank, the river loops to the east, passing Morwellham Quay with its arsenic flues and mineral railway: another thriving scene of past commerce, now preserved for the public by the Dartington Trust. The Tamar returns west to flow by Calstock Quay and, passing under the towering viaduct, built in 1907, arrives at Cotehele. Here a small restored quay with a museum and the *Shamrock* sailing barge, last of her kind on the Tamar, give us an entrancing glimpse of the past industrial heyday along the river: mining, quarrying, limekilns, ochre pits, arsenic flues and brickworks all contributed to that great activity, now long demised. Coal, limestone and ironware were brought up by the barges, which took out the minerals to be transhipped at Plymouth. Now the grey-green Tamar glides between reed beds and high gorges, a haven for herons, curlews and other wading birds, enjoyed by a discerning public and local fishermen, all but forgetful of that thriving tumultuous past.

Below Cotehele the fat, fertile farmlands of the gentler Devon banks are opposed by precipitous wooded Cornish slopes. At Halton Pool, where fish still breed, the Overseers of the Poor in the eighteenth century ruled that no Poor Law apprentice in their care should have salmon to eat more than twice a week. The river, a quarter of a mile wide now, embraces a spur of land which is Botus Fleming parish, with its restored landing-place at Moditonham Quay. This little wharf saw much barge traffic during the nineteenth century: loads of horse-dung swept from Plymouth streets were brought in to manure the farms, and today ploughs still turn up broken ornaments, china dolls, glass bottles and clay pipes.

Rolling onwards the broadening Tamar reaches Cargreen village and quay, with its neat waterside inn and small boats; opposite it the Tavy swells the flood, arriving from Devon. At Saltash the recent road suspension bridge all but dwarfs Brunel's railway bridge of 1853–9 with its elliptical superstructure, now almost a museum piece of Victorian steel brooding over the shipping below. Saltash people, living at the very entrance of Cornwall, are forever conscious of the dynamic power and presence of Plymouth across the bridge; but they show from time to time the same dogmatic attitude that led their Elizabethan predecessors into lawsuits against the Duchy and neighbouring parishes, to protect their water rights. In 1759 Sir James Tillie of Pentillie Castle successfully opposed the 'unjust and iniquitous Saltashers', but Prince George, Duke of Cornwall (later George IV), had to grant their rights to the ferry, oysterage and anchorage in the Tamar, for a very modest rent of £18 a year and a hundred oysters for his Duchy auditor.

Thus the Tamar reaches its wide estuary, with Devonport and Millbay Docks on the Plymouth side, Millbrook, Cremyll and Mount Edgcumbe on the Cornish, and Drake Island in the Sound: as fair a meeting-place of rivers and sea as anywhere, which no doubt prompted the Edgcumbes to move here from Cotehele to build their new house in the sixteenth century.

The Lynher, a major tributary of the Tamar, enters at this confluence. Its name means Long Lake or Pool, and lakelike it is, especially at its broadest after the Tiddy or St Germans river joins it. Rising on Hendra Downs in Altarnun parish, it gathers early strength to define for us the eastern scarp of Bodmin Moor. As a fast-flowing stream it passes below North Hill and South Hill churches, burrowing down through hazels and elmwoods to Newbridge by Callington – which is actually the oldest surviving bridge over it (William Worcester, 1478); its quaint parapets are continually being wrecked by heavy transports. Here some of the loveliest woodlands in Cornwall begin, with salmon and trout sliding over the loud, pebbly shallows and large rock slabs, down to Clapper Bridge by Pillaton – no longer, alas, of clapper construction, having been rebuilt in the sixteenth century. Cadsonbury Iron Age camp lords over the landscape by Newbridge, its precipitous slope fronting the river: it must have been impregnable to attack from the east. Below Notter, where the old bridge stands back from the main road, the river, as Carew said, 'mingleth with the brinish waves'. It soon broadens into a pacific rural estuary, with Ince Castle (eighteenth century) and Shillingham House on the north side, and the Georgian eminence of Antony House on the south. Here the Carew family have been ensconced since the late fifteenth century, and here, in an earlier house, the historian Richard penned his lively and incomparable *Survey of Cornwall*.

The two Looe rivers, the East and West, pass through some of the most attractive and secluded inland scenery of Cornwall. The East, rising near St Cleer on Bodmin Moor, passes down by Liskeard's Moor water estate, driving its deep valley past St Keyne (commemorated by Southey's poem of the Well) and down to a drowned estuary now fast silting up, full of waders and sea birds.

The canal and railway operations along the east bank are still plentifully evident. The Looe Union Canal (1828) ran from Moorswater to Looe and brought agricultural produce and granite from the Cheesewring quarries down to the sea. Much of the stone for the forts

Newbridge over the Lynher

and docks at Plymouth, Portsmouth and Spithead was exported thus, and copper ore from the Caradon mines came this way until the railway took over the trade. Today the hulks of former barges and sailing craft that used to ply here lie rotting in the mud of the creeks.

The West Looe rises at St Pinnock, negotiating a fairly straight course down a deeply forested valley to Herodsfoot, a forgotten hamlet with a nice Victorian bellcoted church by G. E. Street. St Nun's Well lies on its west bank under Pelynt, with an Iron Age fort guarding it. At Watergate and Ten Acre Wood it widens out into an alluvial estuary, with the enigmatic Giant's Hedge earthwork along its south bank.

Thus Looe is reached, its West and East towns connected since 1853 by a 'misshapen bridge of nine arches' (Henderson): the magnificent first bridge here was begun in 1411, to aid travelling between Fowey and Plymouth. It had some fifteen or eighteen arches but was always too narrow. Perhaps it could have been widened, as

Golitha Falls, River Fowey

was done at Wadebridge, but the Victorians decided to tear it down and create another a hundred yards upstream. So it went, along with the little chapel of St Anne which stood on it, another victim of ruthless progress.

The River Fowey is perhaps the most intimately endearing of all Cornish rivers. It springs to life on the high Bodmin Moor, which was formerly, and more properly, called Fowey Moor in its honour. Its source is in the marshes under Brown Willy, the highest hill in Cornwall (*bron*, hill; *ughella*, highest); it traverses two clear miles of virgin moorland among Bronze Age hut circles and tumuli, before encountering modern civilization near Jamaica Inn and Bolventor.

Palmers' Bridge, where it burrows under the A30 main road, by its name betrays its original use by pilgrims *en route* to Spain; the old clapper bridge here was destroyed by a flood in 1880. Down to Draynes (Drayness) is one of the loveliest moorland valley miles in the Duchy; past hill farms with furzy spiky names – Trezibbett,

Harrowbridge, Carkeet, Furswain and Trekievesteps – the Fowey travels in an enclosed world, among ferns and mossy boulders. The thickets of the moor above are, alas, relentlessly retreating before the slow pressure of cultivation, encouraged by EEC grants, from below.

Golitha Falls, renowned as one of Cornwall's interior gems, form a grotto of huge water-smoothed and polished boulders; beyond them the river contorts its way down to Treverbyn Bridge, under monumental beeches, alders and ashes. *Tref*, farm, of Erbyn: an Erbyn was the father of Geraint, sixth-century King of Cornwall and Dumnonia. In the Middle Ages the bridge was important, connecting Bodmin and Liskeard: Bishop Stafford, who had encouraged the building of Looe bridge, granted a further Indulgence for this one, then said to be 'threatening total ruin'. Today the old bridge, perfectly planned and executed, with two lovely arches and moorstone parapet, stands preserved beside a new one carrying the present road.

At Twowatersfoot is the meeting-place of the Fowey and the Loveny, or St Neot, river which comes down from Bolventor ('Bold Venture') to the village of St Neot in its valley bowl beneath the trees, and down another sylvan leafy valley to join its larger neighbour. Through the Glynn valley to Bodmin Road and down to Respryn

Restormel Castle

bridge below the Lanhydrock estate the Fowey continues; the Warleggan or Bedalder river joins it after carving out its valley from the north, descending from Temple Moor and fifteenth-century Panters bridge (originally *Pont Jésus*), in its pocket of poignant woodland beauty amid the Moor.

There has been a bridge at Respryn (*res*, ford; Pryn or Perrin, a personal Celtic name) since at least 1300; the present charmingly proportioned one is fifteenth century, of free granite from the moors. Now a popular spot for picnicking, fishing and walking, Respryn was strategically useful during the Civil War, when King Charles was at Boconnoc and Sir Richard Grenville and his troops at Lanhydrock. At the latter Lord Roberts (later he spelt it Robartes) planted his great avenue of beeches after the Restoration. It is three miles from Respryn down to Lostwithiel Bridge, past the ruins of Restormel Castle, once the seat of the Black Prince.

Thus under alders and sycamores which dip their lowest branches in the high tide, the ancient Stannary town is reached. The bridge is the lowest over the Fowey, and there have been bridges there since

Lerryn Bridge

1190. Visiting Cornwall in 1539, Leland, Henry VIII's chronicler, found the river almost choked by sand and silt, due mainly to mining activities further up; barges could hardly be got up to the quays. A new channel had to be cut and the bridge extended. But as a commercial port Lostwithiel thereafter declined to extinction.

Below Lostwithiel the river matures to a noble watercourse below the well-wooded slopes of Lantyan, Golant and Castle Dore: this was the district Béroul, the twelfth-century Norman-French poet, had in mind when composing his *Romance of Tristan*. On the east bank St Winnow Church stands graciously beside the river, overlooking a green lake on the flood. In the nineteenth century barges and small schooners came up to Lerryn, at the head of its tidal creek, with Plymouth limestone to burn in the limekilns, which are still there. The present bridge was repaired by an Order of Elizabeth I to her Bailiffs and Constable of the Hundred of West. Lerryn was anciently Laryan: perhaps from *lan*, enclosure, or cell, and Rien or Ryan, a forgotten hermit.

Now the Fowey sweeps down to the town that takes its name from it, past Bodinnick with colour-washed cottages climbing a precipitous hill, and the ancient ferry passage, now worked by a car ferry, to Pont Creek and Polruan. Here yachts and pleasure craft mingle with cargo ships of various nations loading china clay. At evening the tide reflects a hundred lights from the port of Fowey, which 'Q', Sir Arthur Quiller-Couch, loved and wrote about in his novels and stories, perhaps the most famous and enjoyable of them being the *The Fabulous History of Troy Town*. And behind us are memories of Rat and Mole and Badger, and Toad of Toad Hall, for Kenneth Grahame, who spent much of his time here messing about in boats, wrote that everlastingly favourite tale *The Wind in the Willows* with the Fowey river in his memory, its currents and seasonal rhythms running through his emotions.

Three miles west of Fowey is the Luxulyan river, which over its short course changes from a moorland stream to a fast torrent scoring a deep, bouldered valley and thence to a slow stream dispersing in the alluvial soil and sand of Par Harbour. The floor of the upper valley was considerably raised by refuse from mining and quarrying over the last two centuries; in 1835 two bridges were dug out at Pont's Mill, some twenty feet below the marshy valley bottom. In the mid eighteenth century the village of Par did not exist; the tide went up to Tywardreath (the House on the Beach) and St Blazey Church, then true to its old name of Landreath – the Cell on the Beach. Par Sands was a dangerous place to cross in the Middle Ages.

Yet now there is Par Harbour, continually dredged to facilitate exports of china clay, and beaches for holiday-makers. Much of the

Treffry Viaduct, River Par

change is due to Joseph Thomas Treffry, that magnate and mining adventurer known as the King of Mid Cornwall, who constructed not only the magnificent viaduct across the upper valley (it carried copper ore from his Fowey Consols mine to Newquay, for export to South Wales and smelting) but also Par Harbour; he owned granite quarries in Luxulyan and china clay workings locally. His imprint is everywhere in the district.

West now to the St Austell river, today running clear, for china clay companies no longer discharge their milky-white sediments into its waters. It murmurs pacifically among the thorns and hazels down past Tregorrick and Kingswood, to run out on Pentewan Sands, where in the time of Thomas Martyn (who published a significant map in 1749) a tidal estuary and a useful port existed.

The River Fal and its sister rivers are the most complex group of waterways in Cornwall, between them draining the Goss Moor, the basins around Truro, Penryn and Falmouth, and the Roseland peninsula. All meet in that wide and majestic highway of salt water known as Carrick Roads or Falmouth Haven, perhaps the best deepwater harbour in the northern hemisphere.

The Fal itself is a child of Roche parish, rising among scrubs and thickets at Pentonvale (*Pen Venten Fala*: the head spring of the Fal). The young stream flows north and west, musing softly through cottage gardens and along beside deep lanes, to reach the bogs and sour marshes of Tregoss Moor. Here a series of dark peaty pools, joining to form an acid lake, presage its descent through open furze and heather-clad land to Retew (Black Ford) and Trerice (Farm of the Ford). Under Damelioc Fort, the Iron Age castle where (in mythical history) Arthur was fathered upon Igerna, it enters china clay country. Once it ran as white as the St Austell river, but there is no mica sediment to discolour it now. Southward it drives through St Stephen-in-Brannel, below the huge tips of Treviscoe, Trethosa and Meledor (scenes indelibly described in Jack Clemo's stark novel *Wilding Graft*), and on to Grampound, where before 1299 the medieval southern Cornish highway crossed it by bridge. At that time it still bore its Cornish name, Pons Mur (Great Bridge), but by 1301 the Norman name Grand Pont came into use.

Three miles further on, the Fal reaches Tregony, like Grampound a decayed borough now reduced to village status. Near Golden Mill is a riverside rock named Haubert ('Haul-boat') to which, Norden wrote in 1584, boats were still tied up to an iron ring. From then on progressive silting-up hampered river traffic, though in 1690 barges could still reach Penvose Quay, two miles below Tregony. A memorable lawsuit dragged on in the late seventeenth century between two cousins named Trevanion, Charles of Cregoe and his namesake Charles of Caerhayes. The former spent a great deal to render the Fal navigable by means of sluices and locks, building eight below Tregony and three above it, but his cousin claimed that the water to his mill at Nansaker was cut off. In time the whole scheme was abandoned, threatening to bankrupt its promoter.

Down through secluded woods of Trewarthenick the slower mature river reaches Ruan Lanihorne, with its disused quay, and Lamorran Woods, where it winds among mudflats at low tide and is a silver-grey pool on the flood. Past the old abandoned house at Ardevora Veor (*ar*, above; *devora*, waters; *mur*, great) which broods sightlessly over the scene, and by the deer park of Tregothnan, it conjoins with the Truro and Tresillian rivers to deepen at a comparatively narrow stretch: King Harry Passage. The old name here was Keybellans; in Cornish, simply Ferry; the passage is immemorial, going back at least to the Bronze Age. Its modern name commemorates King Henry VI. The chapel at Tolverne above it was built in the

Restronguet Creek

early sixteenth century to succour travellers and pilgrims, and at that time the canonization of the ill-used monarch was being put forward. Above the western ferry landing, screened by great trees, is the Georgian house of Trelissick, with its grand pillared neo-Classical portico; the famous gardens are now administered by the National Trust.

Upstream from King Harry, where the Tresillian and Truro rivers flow together, is Malpas (Mauvais Passage), which figures in Béroul as the place where Tristan, disguised as a leper, carried Iseult across the water. She was thus able to swear to her husband, King Mark, that no man except he himself and the leper had ever come between her legs. A fine medieval piece of sophistry.

The Carnon river, flowing in by Devoran, is full of detritus from past and present tin-dredging operations; a secondary stream from Perranarworthal and Perran Wharf, once the scene of great commerce in mining days, meanders among saltgrass-covered flats. Restronguet and Mylor Creeks, St Just Pool and the Perceuil river, which drains the Roseland (*ros*, spur or promontory) all present pacifically enclosed worlds from where the rest of Cornwall is a distant thoroughfare, barely heard, if at all: where by walking a riverside path or shaled foreshore, or by rowing a small boat, it is still possible to find a rare and blessed silence.

And so to Carrick Roads, which, since Falmouth became a packet station for Spain, the West Indies and American colonies in 1688, has been an anchorage for great ships of all nations. It has declined over the last fifty years, but the dry dock is profitable, and Carrick Road is a yachtsman's joy; Henry VIII's twin castles, St Mawes and Pendennis, still stand guard over the estuary; St Anthony light flashes its warnings to all craft, and the wide ocean highways stretch beyond.

The beautiful and (commercially) unused Helford river flows down from Gweek, hidden among oak groves under Celtic forts, down to its wide, cliff-guarded mouth below Falmouth. Its stretches of riverside are remarkable for their variety of vegetation: rich farmland, ancient native woods, exotic gardens at Durgan, and cottage plots full of fuchsias, hydrangeas and familiar flowers at Helford village itself.

> Helford River, Helford River,
> Blessed may ye be!
> We sailed up Helford River
> By Durgan from the sea.
> O to hear the hawser chain
> Rattle by the ferry there!
> Dear, and shall we come again to Bosahan
> By wood and water fair?

So wrote Q, a passionate yachtsman.

Gweek, anciently Wyke (i.e. *vicus*: Latin, town or settlement) dealt in tin as far back as Celtic and Roman times. A charming clapper bridge of the sixteenth century still serves as a footpath over the stream. Merther, on the north bank a mile or two below, unloaded timber ships from Norway during the eighteenth and nineteenth centuries and did a brisk trade in oysters. Scotts Quay and Port Navas were the main centres of the Helford oyster fisheries, and both Helford and Gillan, at the very mouth, saw a great deal of trade including the export of tin.

The Cober river plunges down the valley below Helston, having risen near Hangman's Barrow on Carnmemnellis Moor, and feeds

Carrick Roads

the Loe Pool. Its name derives from *gover*, stream. The upper valley being a great tin-streaming district in the Middle Ages, Helston grew up as its centre, becoming a Stannary (tin-coining) town in the early fourteenth century. As a result of the sanding-up of the Cober mouth, creating the Loe Bar and Pool, Gweek became the main port for Helston about the same time. The Pool is the largest lake in Cornwall: a quiet and beautiful but sometimes frightening scene – several drownings have been recorded, some recently; at least one ghost is reputed to walk down and disappear into the deep, cold waters. Loe trout are a proud type unto themselves, delicious to eat. A sluice and culvert through the Bar now control the flow of the Cober to the sea, but at times of flood in the past the burgesses presented leathern purses to the squire of Penrose, above the Pool, for permission to cut through the Bar. Some of these ancient mementoes are still kept above the hearth at Penrose House.

The Hayle river rises sixteen miles east of the town which shares its name (meaning simply 'estuary'), under Polcrebo Down in Crowan parish. After wandering down to the great pond on Clowance estate amid wooded parkland, it turns west to pursue an almost hidden course through farmland, as rural and unassuming a watercourse as any. It reaches Relubbus (*res*, ford; Lehoubes, another Norman lord) and turns north through Enys Woods to Porthcallum. A *porth* name here would imply navigation in early times (*porth*, landing-place); if so, it must have been before 1330, for Leland gives that as the date of building St Erth Bridge, a mile or two lower. The area was rich in tin,

Clapper Bridge on Bodmin Moor

and the presence of a small square fort at Bosence would indicate Roman interest in its trade.

St Erth was on the medieval highway to the Mount, Mousehole and therefore Santiago; the bridge over the ford there was a great improvement, the most important one until it was superseded by the Hayle causeway in 1835. By 1603, it being in a sad state of repair, a rate of £170 was imposed on the parishioners to repair it, which provoked a 'general murmuring among the people'. There was continual trouble in getting it repaired. A canal was constructed in the eighteenth century to reach St Erth, the river having by then silted up badly.

The passage across the sands at Hayle had always been dangerous, and the famous case of John Wesley being almost trapped and drowned there in his coach is only one of many. The causeway and two bridges cost £5,000, which was recovered by charging rates of ½d for each foot passenger, 2d for a cart and 6d for a coach or chaise. The wide, sandy estuary of the Hayle provides a fascinating study in marine life, flora and fauna; it is a continuing heritage of herons, gulls, terns, curlews, sea-spurge, marram grass, sea holly and so much else. Long, pleasant beaches along each side attract holiday-makers, who are never crammed together.

The port of Hayle, full of industrial archaeological remains, is a living museum piece. Lelant, on the opposite shore with its ancient church of St Uny above the sands, was actually the main port on the estuary until the seventeenth century, when St Ives developed as a fishing harbour. So the Hayle reaches its broad confluence with the sea, with Godrevy Lighthouse on one side and St Ives town light on the other. There is a proliferation of caravan and chalet sites along the Towans (sandhills) towards Gwithian; these, with the old Celtic foundations of Phillack, St Ives and Lelant churches evident on the landscape, and the empty mausoleum of Hayle power station, closed in 1971, produce an interesting if uneasy combination of effects. At Gwithian flows in a stream called in Leland's time Dowr Connor (Connor Water); on the east is Connor Downs, named from the great medieval manor lying below it. The legend of the ancient city of Connor, said to lie beneath the sandhills, may represent lingering memories of a port some way inland, for *connor* means haven in Irish, and there were Irish landings all around the coast in this district from the third century onwards.

The massive basalt, greenstone and slate cliffs of the north coast begin at Navax Point and continue for seventy miles or more to Morwenstow, broken only by a few rivers, two of which have real estuaries: the Gannel and the Camel. The Red River runs down from under the great rocks of Carn Brea and its neolithic and Iron Age forts, still rufous from the soil of mine workings. Reswythen Bridge by St Euny Church was undermined by tinners in 1301. The river, after negotiating the marshes beyond Redruth, runs out among the docks and quays of Portreath.

The Gannel ('Channel') is another river of memories rather than of daily use today. From medieval times it was of importance to Truro, bringing in timber, salt and coal from Bristol, South Wales and Ireland; the goods were taken overland by trains of packhorses and mules. It participated in the shipbuilding boom of the last century, its busy yards on the north bank near Tregunnel providing small schooners and barges.

Rising seven miles east at Fraddon, it flows quietly down through Ennis Woods and Kestle Mill, from which, until the last two years of the nineteenth century, the district around Newquay and St Columb was supplied with stone-ground wholemeal flour. Sixteenth-century Trerice, home of the Arundell family, is built on the high ground overlooking it from the north. Old Trevemper Bridge (1613) remains in good preservation, immediately above the concrete modern bridge of 1925. Former warehouses nearby used to store corn and manure. Above Trevemper is Gwills, perhaps the Guelit where St Crantoc disembarked from Wales around AD 520 to begin his ministry; he is of course commemorated at Crantock, above the mouth of the Gannel.

Now the river takes wide slow loops among marshes and reedbeds which are covered only by high spring tides; the dense trees descending gently on the southern bank are opposed by a precipitously wooded cliff on the north, into which new villas have been built. The river reaches a deep lagoon among the sands at its mouth, Crantock beach almost closing it off from the sea. The high-banked sands stretch west to Kelsey Head and are a marvellous playground for holiday-makers; here the rollers bear in their ever-increasing devotees of the great sport of surfing. From the vantage point of Pentire (Head Land) is a wonderfully arresting view of river and foreshore, with Crantock village and its spired church above (its beautifully restored interior a great joy to behold): a prospect marred only by the perversity of planners in allowing an obtrusive caravan park on the high ground near the village.

The River Camel rises on Bodmin Moor, coming down from Hendraburnick to Camelford, where since the fourteenth century a bridge has superseded the ford. A complex of small moorland streams moving through narrow valleys and medieval woodlands drains this area; there are delightful clapper bridges, the rock-strewn gorge of the Devil's Jump and ancient farmhouses and hamlets. 'Camel' derives from *cam*, crooked or curved, and *heyle*, estuary: an accurate description of the mouth. But until 1870 the main river had the Irish name Allen, said to derive from the Irish *alain*, beautiful, and Irish influence is certainly evident on Ogam stones in the district. The name Allen now attaches, erroneously, to the upper tributary, properly the Laine, which flows from under Delabole through St Teath and St Mabyn – though the description is justified, for the valley is indeed very lovely, especially at bluebell time. Road-widening schemes threatened recently to ruin it but have mercifully been stopped.

At Worthyvale near Camelford stands the seventh-century stone to Catrinus, son of Magarus; by 1602 a tradition, reported by Carew, had grown that the name was Atry and that it commemorated Arthur; nearby is Slaughterbridge, where Arthur was believed to have received his mortal wound. It is easy to see how legends grow out of flimsy, misinterpreted evidence, but the tradition that Arthur, the great British hero, will one day come again was strong in Cornwall during the Middle Ages.

A fast-flowing tributary from under the rocky vertebrae of Roughtor Hill negotiates the dangerous Stannon marshes, passing extinct quarries, Bronze Age huts and circles, to join the main river above Gam Bridge. Here a great waterburst in 1847 swept away the old bridge: a huge wall of water roared down the valley one hot summer afternoon, destroying or choking all the bridges over the Camel except Helland and Wadebridge, the two oldest; more than a year later straw, mud and hay still interwreathed the trees along the riverside.

The de Lank river enters below Poley Bridge, taking its name from the Norman manor of Lank. Rising beyond Roughtor, it twists among hill farms down to Bolatherick, near where King Arthur's Hall, a rectangular enclosure of earthen banks and granite slabs, stands above its northern bank. This may be a medieval pound. Under rustic clapper bridges at Bradford and Delphy, and below the great granite quarries of Hantergantick and de Lank it flows, before joining the Camel.

Blisland village now rises above, its church and green shrouded among high beeches. Fourteenth-century Helland Bridge, in a hidden rural pocket below the moor, is of solid moorstone with four arches: nine feet wide, it has never had to be widened. Southwards the Camel now moves through woods at Colquite (the Wooded Peak) and Pencarrow (Deer Head), down to Dunmere (the Great Fort) and a widening wooded valley where the priors of Bodmin had a weir, from which the townsfolk often poached salmon. A chapel to St Anne stood at the east end of the bridge.

Turning north-west and now gathering speed, the river passes beneath the square Roman fort at Tregear by Nanstallon (*nans*,

Blisland

valley; 'of the Allen'). Grogley Wood is an angler's paradise, where mayflies, in season, flit over brown, translucent pools.

The course of the Camel now parallels the track of the former Bodmin–Wadebridge railway, opened in 1834 and closed in 1979: it was the third line in all Britain. A ramblers' route is now being created along the permanent way by the County Council, ensuring access to some of the most exquisite inland scenery of Cornwall. At Pendavy, two miles further down, the Laine (Allen) meets the main river; here the priors had a manor house, chapel and wharf in pre-Reformation times.

Now the valley widens out to watermeadows flooded at high spring tides, and the river develops wide, meandering loops. Egloshayle (the Church on the Estuary), traded in Irish gold and Cornish tin four thousand years ago and prospered until the building of the bridge below it in 1468.

Before Wade Bridge was built, a dangerous ford or ferry had to be negotiated there. John Loveybond, Vicar of Egloshayle, determined to improve matters: he obtained stone from Penmayne in St Minver, and Bishop Courtney issued an Indulgence. In Leland's words, 'Good people putting ther help there to, finished it with xvii great uniforme arches.' 320 feet long, it has been widened three times to accommodate traffic, which still besieges it in summer. Chapels stood at each end until the Dissolution.

A widening but very tidal flood, the Camel now bears down between disused quays to where the little Amble stream enters among marshes and a valuable bird sanctuary. At Cant Hill (*cant*, elbow or corner) it turns due north (this is the *cam* or crooked element of the name), past the now silent Camel quarries on the south bank, with their derelict engine-house and slate-cutters' floors.

The track of the Padstow–Wadebridge railway, closed in 1967, now provides a footpath giving magnificent views of the estuary and of the muddy tidal creeks, naturalists' joys, up and down it. Little Petherick Creek brings in the last tributary from St Columb Downs, past the tidal gristmill pool at Sea Mills; in 1899 the grand curved iron railway bridge, now part of the footpath, closed off the creek to shipping.

Padstow, today reviving as a port, and Rock village, with its

Rock village and quay

Hawker's Cove, Camel estuary

Duchy quay and many yachts, look at each other over a mile and a half of tempting golden sands at low tide. The 1337 Black Rock Ferry passage is now worked by large motor ferries; the Doom (more properly Dun) Bar, which has swallowed the bones of so many ships, almost blocks off the harbour entrance. Camel estuary lime sand has supplied north and mid Cornwall for many centuries, but the bars show no signs of decreasing.

Between the brooding cliffs of Stepper Point, quarried away to moderate the wind for sailing ships, and the tall bluff of Pentire Head, the Celtic Sea clashes with the estuary waters; great rollers crash on the basalt rocks of Pentire, where until 1857 silver and lead were mined. Thus the Camel finds her destination, carrying, as do all her sister rivers, age-long memories and cautious hopes for the future.

3 Market Towns and Boroughs

The towns of Cornwall are none of them large, and most of them date from the Middle Ages. The oldest, Bodmin, is pre-tenth century and grew up around its Celtic monastery; the largest, Camborne-Redruth, is mainly a creation of the mining boom of the eighteenth and nineteenth centuries. No single town dominates the Cornish scene, though Truro, the cathedral town and administrative centre, has recently greatly expanded with increased shopping and commerce.

Launceston, gateway to Cornwall in Norman times, has never lost its particularly Cornish character. Its medieval aspects remain in the ruins of Robert of Mortain's eleventh-century castle, looming over the town as a reminder of its great past. The impressive South Gate is still there, admitting one car at a time; the bank or town wall between it and Northgate can still be followed. On the castle walls in 1574 the recusant priest St Cuthbert Mayne was hanged, drawn and quartered; an annual Pilgrimage procession now carries his relics to the castle. In the dreaded dank and filthy county prison, still extant within the castle wall, the Quaker George Fox and so many others suffered down the centuries.

Architecturally rewarding, Launceston offers us above all the magnificent church of St Mary Magdalene, its exterior covered with noble carvings executed in that difficult stone, Cornish granite. On the south side of the market square is the old coaching inn the White Hart; its Norman archway came from the ruined priory of St Thomas below the town. Elegant Georgian houses, one containing the town museum, stand on Castle Hill. The Methodist church has a grand spire and competes with the parish church, a hundred yards away; there is an imposing 1887 town hall and a solid guildhall of 1881.

The original monastic foundation was at St Stephen's, opposite modern Launceston, across the valley of the Kensey; in 930 a college of secular canons was established there, and called Lan-stephenston. But with the building of the castle, the market moved across to the new growing town (then known as Dunheved). It was the beginning of St Stephen's decline, and the building of the priory of St Thomas about 1140 completed the process. Even its name, corrupted to Launceston, in time became attached to the new borough. Around St Thomas' Church, down beside the Kensey, are rich archaeological remains. There is a delightful little packhorse bridge, a Gothic umbrella of 1829, with the stump of the old market cross of the borough of Newport, which, like Launceston itself, sent two members to Westminster before the Reform Bill of 1832.

Callington, sixteen miles south of Launceston, is on the downs above the Lynher river and grew up in the fourteenth and fifteenth

The South Gate, Launceston

centuries on the wool trade. Until 1832 it also had two MPs. Its fine granite church was built around 1430, though until recently it was a chapelry of South Hill, two miles away. Callington decayed during the last two centuries but is now receiving the benefit of some new, tasteful developments.

Liskeard is of Celtic origin (*lys*, court or seat of justice; of Kerryt, a local chief or king). After the building of Horsebridge and then Newbridge (Gunnislake), it prospered through the wool trade with Tavistock, the centre of Devon serge-making, and also became the main mineral market in south-east Cornwall; its market house, coinage hall and prison stood on one central site, now covered by a modern department store. In the late sixteenth century it had about a thousand inhabitants, including twelve bakers and ten shoemakers. The castle, if such it was (it may have been a fortified manor house), is said to have been built by Richard, King of the Romans and Earl of Cornwall, but was allowed to fall down. Police houses now occupy part of its site.

Befitting the town's expansion during the fifteenth century, the church is elaborate, the second largest in Cornwall after Bodmin, with impressive granite arcades and surviving Norman work. The town sent the usual two MPs to London and became known as 'the Model Borough', having a minimum of corruption, though the Eliot family of St Germans controlled it. Apparently the voters invariably did what was expected of them, resisting all blandishments.

A mid-nineteenth-century expansion took place as a result of the opening of mines on Caradon Moor above the town; the Parade was then built, presenting us with its fine Georgian and Victorian buildings. The canal and Looe–Caradon railway took ore and granite down to Looe for shipment. Today Liskeard thrives steadily, happily bypassed by the main A30 traffic.

Lostwithiel town nestles in a green bowl under its surrounding hills. The old lower part of the town is quiet and free from heavy traffic. The church of St Bartholomew, with its marvellous octagonal Breton-type spire, and the frontage of the old Duchy Palace buildings by the river, exude a serenity born of an illustrious past: for Lostwithiel was the capital of Cornwall in the thirteenth and fourteenth centuries. Richard, King of the Romans, acquired Restormel Castle, a mile off, and improved it; his son Edmund, succeeding him as Earl of Cornwall, built the Duchy Palace with its shire hall, exchequer and coinage hall, where tin was assayed and duty paid thereon. Here also was the Stannary gaol, where languished prisoners convicted under Stannary law. The Cornish tin-miners, under their Convocation or Stannary Parliament, were virtually a state within a state, making their own laws by royal charter, exempt from

London-imposed taxes. The Black Prince, first Duke of Cornwall, improved the castle, and on his visits there trade was brought to Lostwithiel by tenants and burgesses doing him homage and presenting petitions. But after his death both Restormel and the town decayed; the Fowey silted up, and barges could no longer get up to its quays. By 1801 there were only 743 people there, living in 125 houses.

But some fine Georgian houses were built in North Street, Duke Street and the Parade, and the arrival of the railway in 1854 brought increased trade. Today Lostwithiel has a useful shopping centre, some interesting inns, an enormous and aesthetically outrageous square dried-milk factory, a magnificent Methodist church with cupola, and a well-used though poorly designed community centre.

The history of Bodmin, remarked John Betjeman, is long and sad. It was an important site in the Bronze Age and Celtic times, just off the Camel–Fowey trading route, surrounded by Iron Age forts. The building of St Petroc's second monastery there in the sixth century

Lostwithiel Bridge

laid the foundations for the medieval town, which grew up after Padstow (the first monastic settlement) was burned by the Vikings in 981; from then on the abbots and priors ruled from Bodmin. The name derives from *bos*, a dwelling, and *menegh*, monks.

The town was undoubtedly the greatest religious centre in Cornwall in medieval times; the Augustinians took over the original Celtic monastery, and the Franciscans built a friary there in the thirteenth century, on what is now Mount Folly. There were numerous chapels and two leper houses, one of which, St Lawrence's, became the county asylum and now mental hospital. Above all, the shrine of St Petroc attracted hundreds of pilgrims each year.

The importance of these holy relics cannot be underestimated. When a Breton monk stole them and took them to his own foundation at Saint-Méen, the general outcry resulted in an appeal to Henry I of England, who, as overlord of Brittany, ordered the return

Bodmin: Mount Folly Square and Law Courts

of the bones. The priceless ivory casket in which he returned them can still be seen behind plate glass in the church. Also surviving are the early medieval Bodmin Gospels, with their tenth-century records of manumissions, the freeing of slaves, at the shrine.

The church itself was rebuilt in the fifteenth century, as were so many others, bringing in the Perpendicular style in place of the Norman; 460 people contributed to the work, employing twenty masons and costing £268.17s.19½d. Many gave their skills free or donated materials: Bodmin was not to be outdone by other Cornish towns. A ruined chapel to St Thomas à Becket (1377) stands in the churchyard, but the original priory has disappeared under a park and recreation ground.

Bodmin suffered extensively from the Black Death; some fifteen hundred people died there, including two canons and the prior. But the town continued to grow slowly and was one of the chief centres of the Cornish rebellions of 1497 and 1545. Thomas Flamank, a lawyer, was a leader of the first and was executed at Tyburn; Nicholas Boyer, mayor of the town, was hanged for his part in the second.

The town declined after the Reformation and the dismemberment of the monasteries; it revived with the turnpike road established over the moors from Launceston, leading to the Assizes being held there; it then gained the grand Classically styled court buildings, the judges' chambers opposite and the prison with its tremendous gateway. It also acquired two railway stations (Southern and Great Western) and the inescapable beacon, an obelisk to General Sir Walter Raleigh Gilbert, who served in India.

After 1900 the main flow of trade and commerce bypassed Bodmin; it was depressed in the 1940s and 50s, and the town council's overspill agreement with the GLC sought to inject new prosperity. The Crown Court (formerly the Assizes) is now to move to Truro. However, community life is vigorous, and Bodmin, still conscious of its great past, continues to hold its own.

Camelford, ten miles to the north, is an unpretentious but harmonious little town, with interesting slate buildings along the A39 road which dips down to the valley and its bridge. Despite being a parliamentary borough with two members, it grew only very slowly; perhaps the moorland farms about it were too poor to bring enough trade. Neither the coming of the turnpike road in 1795 nor that of the North Cornwall Railway in 1893 seemed greatly to affect it. Among its better buildings are the Earl of Darlington Inn, the 1806 town hall, and the Methodist church with quaintly stepped Sunday school. Today the town benefits from the tourist trade and the landscape of Arthurian associations, and Roughtor Hill, one of Cornwall's moorland attractions, bring motorists and hikers.

Wadebridge was never a borough; it grew up mainly as a result of the building of its bridge, although until recently its parish church remained a mile or more away at St Breock. The wool trade must always have been important to the town. The legend of building the bridge on packs of wool, however, portrays a symbolic rather than an actual truth, for successive widenings of the bridge have found no evidence of it.

Trade from the quays below the bridge flourished in the nineteenth century; scores of barges came up daily to unload lime-sand from the lower Camel estuary, and the Wadebridge–Bodmin railway took it inland to the farmers. Granite from the moorland quarries was worked on the quays, then shipped out to build various London bridges, docks at Singapore and Gibraltar, and the Eddystone lighthouse, thus giving the name Eddystone to a quayside road. China clay from Wenford Bridge was also exported; a variety of cargoes, including timber, groceries and bricks, were brought in by schooners on the high tide. But the coastal shipping declined with the arrival of the Southern Railway, in 1895, and now all maritime activity on the quays has ceased. Wadebridge is today a busy shopping centre and has a few notable buildings, including the Moleworth Arms, an old coaching inn with courtyard and former stables.

Six miles westwards over what was the turnpike road (a tollgate house is still preserved on it) is St Columb Major, 'a great parish and a little market towne' to quote Norden. Its market dates from 1333 and is still active; its church was rebuilt in the fifteenth century to include the Arundel Chapel, with its fine memorials; the family, staunch Catholics, who later paid dearly for their loyalty to Rome, held the manor of Lanherne nearby. A chantry chapel attached to the church, housing for secular priests, was destroyed by fire in 1701. St Columb may have been dedicated to the great Columba of Iona, though local legend says that she was a virgin martyred at Ruthvoes in the parish.

Along the narrow, claustrophobic streets of this slate-built town (which previous to the building of the bypass was a nightmare to motorists) are some unusual Victorian edifices including Bank House (Venetian Gothic by William White), the exotically excessive Barclay's Bank, Regency-styled Liberal and Conservative Clubs staring at each other in the square, and the Red Lion Inn where James Polkinhorne, the Cornish champion wrestler, is commemorated. (At the Silver Ball inn each year, a hurling ball is ceremoniously dipped in ale after the Hurling.) In the valley below the town is the old Rectory, uniquely moated; an earlier building there was besieged by tinners during riots in 1309.

As a town, St Austell is of comparatively recent growth, due to

The bridge at Wadebridge

mining and china clay activities since 1750. Before that it was a quiet village, but with as fine a church as any in Cornwall; it was the churchtown for a large, rich parish which included many sheep farms, the great open-cast tin-mine of Carclaze, and Pentewan, then a busy port with quarries producing fine stone for church rebuilding. During the eighteenth century other mines opened in the district; by 1772 Polgooth employed over a thousand men, women and children and had a Newcomen atmospheric engine pumping water out of its fifty shafts.

Cookworthy's discoveries led to the production of china clay in the district, and gradually pits opened up to produce the fine white powder for Staffordshire potteries; the town expanded dramatically as a result. Today St Austell is the metropolis of the clay industry and its many ancillary trades and services; the landscape around it is dominated by huge tips of waste sand, many now grassed over. It is a prosperous industry, with good industrial relations.

Truro

The town itself has undergone considerable redevelopment, juxtaposing new buildings with the old; the Georgian White Hart Hotel and Renaissance-style town hall contrast with the inevitable blank-walled Tesco store, but the shopping precinct with cinemas and multi-storey car-park is pleasant enough. With arts and sports centres, secondary schools, sixth-form and technical colleges, it is a lively place for young and old.

The position of Truro has been of great significance since earliest times. An Iron Age fort stands above the meeting of roads and rivers there; the name is obscure but seems to contain the Cornish element *try*, three. Triuru, 1198, and Trewiru, 1201, are recorded: probably Three Rivers or Three Roads. The southern route through Cornwall could avoid Truro only by using King Harry Passage. The Kenwyn and Allen rivers meet at the town, with the Tresillian joining a mile or two below.

With a charter of 1153 and a market near the quays, Truro grew steadily in the shadow of its Norman castle (now entirely removed, though remains of the walls were found in 1840). The establishment of the Dominican friary at Newham, now the south part of the town, led to the draining of marshes and the creation of some impressive buildings, which fell into disuse after the Reformation; by 1700 only part of the church was left.

Meanwhile, about 1320, Truro had become a coinage town and tin centre; its maritime trade grew, despite a series of catastrophic plagues during and after the Black Death period. Norden (1584) described it as 'a pretty compacted towne, well peopled and with wealthy marchauntes' and said that it exceeded Penryn for 'providence, traffic and good Government'. But Celia Fiennes (1699) called it 'a ruinated disregarded place' – such effects had the swings and roundabouts of national and international trade. However, new techniques in mining brought money into Truro, which during the 1750s and later decades became the cultural and political metropolis of Cornwall.

The Robartes family built their Great House (now demolished to provide a chainstore) in Boscawen Street; Classical-styled houses like the Mansion House and Princes House were built (they now house offices); also the Red Lion, a splendid coaching inn (now also unhappily pulled down), Georgian Lemon Street, named after a local mining tycoon and benefactor, Regency Strangeways Terrace and Walsingham Place – delightful additions still mercifully with us. The infirmary of 1799, gift of Lord de Dunstanville of Tehidy, a theatre, Philharmonic Society, assembly rooms, the Royal Institution of Cornwall, and the noble granite city hall in Boscawen Street, all followed as the town prospered. Neville Burnard's great statue of the

Truro: Cathedral Square

Truro explorer Richard Lander is set on a magnificent Doric column commanding the façades of Lemon Street.

The climax to all this was the building of J. L. Pearson's Anglican cathedral (1880–1909). The architect was influenced by Breton and French usages; rising from narrow streets without lawns on three sides, it can be compared with the cathedral of St Pol de Léon. It incorporates the south aisle of the former church of St Mary's, one of Cornwall's ornate treasures. The addition of those three perfect Gothic spires, seen floating above the morning mist or discovered stabbing the sky above the high buildings about it, was a master stroke of celestial effect.

Truro has lately suffered too much at the hands of developers; commercial pressures have unduly influenced planners and their committees. Depressingly featureless blocks have been permitted in Boscawen Street, at odds with the old granite setts (paving blocks) and Victorian buildings. Pydar Street, decaying in the 1950s and 60s, has revived with the coming of large chainstores – including a new, acceptable, slate-faced Marks & Spencer's, and another Tesco's, whose functional concrete boxes have defaced too many old towns. In 1969 a new County Hall above the town extended the local government empire; the modern church of Our Lady and St Piran adds a touch of Byzantine colour. New arcades of shops proliferate. Whether Truro can go on growing, probably at the expense of other Cornish towns, is a question now being widely asked.

Redruth and Camborne were, like St Austell, creations mainly of the mining age, though both have fine churches built on Celtic foundations. Norden described Camborne as 'a churche standing among barren hills'; the name derives from *cam*, curved or crooked, and *bron*, a hill or breast. The original patron saint was Meriasek of Brittany, the subject of the town's saint's play; today he shares the dedication with St Martin.

Many famous mines have been worked over the centuries in the parish, including Dolcoath, Carnkye, Trevenson, Cook's Kitchen and the Carn Brea complex; more than eighty were at work at one time or another in Camborne and adjoining Illogan parishes, and the mouldering granite chimneystacks of their pumping engines still brood over the landscape, reminders of that great past. Today only South Crofty, within the town area, and Wheal Pendarves, a mile or two away, work on, and even they are under threat of closure.

Outside the public library stands a fine bronze statue of Richard Trevithick, the town's most famous engineer, whose perfection of high-pressure steam resulted in the second Industrial Revolution. He is also commemorated in the popular Cornish folksong 'Going up Camborne Hill':

> Going up Camborne Hill, coming down,
> Going up Camborne Hill, coming down:
> The horses stayed still, the wheels went around,
> Going up Camborne Hill, coming down.

The horse-drawn vehicles stood still in amazement whilst Trevithick drove his steam locomotive past them, up the hill to Beacon.

Another verse remembers the white-stockinged women workers of William Bickford's safety-fuse factory at Tuckingmill, on the east side of the town:

> White stockings, white stockings she wore,
> White stockings, white stockings she wore:
> White stockings she wore, the same as before,
> Going up Camborne Hill, coming down.

Bickford's fuses contributed greatly to the safety of miners all over the world. A plaque to his name, dated 1831, is to be seen on the factory wall.

In the town is a notable Literary Institute, now an Age Concern centre: a brave 1829 venture in granite with Tuscan pillars and wings. On the campus of Cornwall Technical College is the Camborne School of Mines, world specialists in mining education, and the Institute of Cornish Studies. Camborne built two remarkable Methodist churches, Wesley Church, with its cream and blue façade, and the Centenary Methodist Church of 1839, with its beautifully kept interior. The Holman engineering works, producing mining and drilling equipment, is now part of a global organization, and employed a large workforce. It recently suffered from large-scale redundancies. An easier bustle now fills the town's shopping centre since the A30 was carried past it along a six-mile long bypass.

Redruth, said Norden, was in 1584 'a hamlet annexed to Uni-Redruth, where are manie tynn works, both streame and lode works'. Of these enterprises now only Tolgus, a working museum showing the nineteenth-century process of sorting and crushing tin, is active. But evidence remains that the town was a cut above Camborne, being the place where mine captains and the better classes lived.

'Uni' is St Euny, the mother church of Redruth, a pretty granite village in a wooded hollow below Carn Brea. Its fine Georgian church has a fifteenth-century tower. The name Redruth comes from *res*, ford, and *ruth*, red, or possibly from *dreweth*, druid. The whole valley of the Red River, descending from the moor to Portreath, is full of former attle (waste heaps) and disused adits. Pednandrea (End of the Town) mine still raises two-thirds of its ivy-covered stack over the hillside. About a hundred other workings went on in and around the town, some rich, many unprofitable.

Today the town benefits greatly from light industry. The main street plunges down to an inconvenient crossing; the 1850 town hall, with clocktower, and the elegant Wesleyan church of 1830 stand out boldly against the uninspiring glass fronts and a concrete post office. Down a side street is Murdoch House, where the Scot William Murdoch made the first gas engine in 1784; in 1792 he was the first man to light his house with gas.

Throughout the Middle Ages and until the eighteenth century, Helston was a coinage town and the western metropolis of Cornish mining. It was the focal point of trade for Meneage and the Lizard district; the breadth of its main street and its many noble buildings bespeak its past dominance.

There was an Iron Age settlement, probably just north of the

Fore Street, Redruth

present town, at Hellescoth – the Old Court. In Domesday the manor is called Henliston: the Saxon *tun* (town) being added to the Celtic *hen*, old, and *lys*, court, indicating a growing influx of English. Forty 'alemen' then resided there: they paid their taxes in ale. King John (1201) granted the town's first charter, and a castle was built in that century by Edmund, Earl of Cornwall, though nothing now remains of it.

By the end of the thirteenth century the Cober river below the town was dammed by the Loe Bar, and the borough turned to Gweek as its port; the town gallows were set up there. Despite steady growth, Norden called Helston a decayed town, and it apparently suffered from the trading depressions of that time. In 1547 the officious William Body, lessee of the archdeaconry of Cornwall, was murdered, sparking off a minor rebellion; Helstonians rose in defence of their Catholic religion and their statues and images, which Body had been destroying.

Trade revived in the next century, and over two hundred 'spalliers' (working tinners) were recorded in or near the town. Carew wrote that Godolphin Bal (mine) employed three hundred persons. From 1641 to 1801 the population rose from 803 to 2,241. Helston supplied six Stannators to the Cornish Convocation of Tinners, which last met in 1752.

The fine coinage hall, on the site of a medieval chapel, the spacious Georgian church, the Bowling Green with Gothic gateway, the 1839 town hall, the sixteenth-century Angel Hotel and many other proud buildings, set near intricate narrow lanes and cuttings, present a town memorable to visit. A marble memorial to Henry Trengrouse, inventor of the life-saving rocket apparatus, is in the churchyard. Before its rebuilding the church contained the Chapel of St Michael, in which the Guild of Cordwainers had their own altar; their strict, God-fearing rules have come down to us and are remarkably like more recent Friendly Society and Trades Union constitutions, full of concern for the welfare of both masters and servants.

Penzance (the Holy Head) owes its name to a small promontory below which a dock was built in the fifteenth century. A medieval chapel stood on it; the town's arms, the head of John the Baptist on a salver, are a visual pun on the name. Apart from a few fishermen's cottages on the Alwarton (Alverton) estate, there was little there in the Middle Ages; Marazion and Mousehole dwarfed the settlement. But all three were burned by the Spaniards in 1598 as a reprisal for the defeat of the Armada. The rebuilt Penzance obtained a charter from James I and began to grow with increased shipping and the tin trade. By 1801 there were 694 houses there. The grand granite market house of 1838 replaced the old guildhall and coinage hall; before it stands the statue of Sir Humphrey Davy, the great chemist and inventor of the miner's safety lamp. Madron was the mother church of Penzance; in 1836 old St Mary's in Chapel Street was pulled down to make way for a new Georgian-type parish church with a gallery.

To Penzance in the early nineteenth century came invalids, bathers and walkers to enjoy the mild climate and invigorating sea air; gracious Classical terraces of stucco grew up, the sub-tropical

Coinagehall Street, Helston

Morrab Gardens were laid out, and the public library, municipal hall and colourful Egyptian House were built. The coming of the railway brought the town and all West Penwith within reach of London; later in the nineteenth century workers' excursions to Land's End from the North of England became popular.

Today the town is a thriving shopping and holiday centre, with a long sea-front from which to view the splendours of Mount's Bay and St Michael's Mount. Traffic is obnoxious in summer. The harbour does not now handle fish but is the mainland port for the Scillonian run, though increasing air traffic to the islands now goes from the heliport on the east of the town.

4 Fishing Ports and Harbours

Many and varied are the reasons for the growth of ports around the Cornish coast. The estuaries, of course, have been used for fishing and trading from earliest times, and some sea ports, like Marazion, are of great antiquity. Others flourished mainly in the Middle Ages. Some rose to prosper on pilchards, some on tin; some are now, despite their great past, hardly worth the name of ports.

The first on the north coast, Bude, is perhaps the strangest of all. It is a most unpromising place, where a tiny river runs out among sands which break a long line of awesome cliffs. Yet in the eighteenth and nineteenth centuries Bude Haven supplied a large area untouched by main roads and railways. It built schooners and had agents and merchants engaged in a considerable seaborne trade, bringing in coal, ironware, timber and domestic supplies and exporting local corn.

The original name was Bude Haven; at a hermitage on Chapel Rock an anchorite tended a light to guide medieval seafarers. The village grew up on the west side of the bay, and in 1820 the canal, an ambitious undertaking, was opened. One branch went to the Tamar, the other to beyond Holsworthy in Devon. There are no locks but railed inclines up which barges with small wheels on their keels were pulled, taking the limesand of the bay to the farms inland to sweeten the soil. The old village expanded with warehouses and inns; the canal operated until 1884.

Meanwhile the railway had reached the area, and on the north side of the bay, near Poughill churchtown, hotels and guesthouses began to appear; soon the splendid beaches regularly received summer holiday-makers. Bude lifeboat performed much valorous work during the last century, assisting vessels making for the Haven amid terrifying seas. Sometimes they were huge East Indiamen like the ill-fated *Bencoolen*, sometimes local coasters like the *Elizabeth Scown*, lost in 1877 with the lifeboat itself. Today few boats use Bude, though on the lower canal elderly vessels are renovated for maritime museums.

Bocastle Harbour is built in a deep ravine between towering cliffs

Bude Canal

and was in use before the sixteenth century. In 1861 Walter White, Librarian to the Royal Society, wrote after a visit, 'On each side the space is occupied by warehouses, workshops, shipyards, timber yards, and all the appliances of a busy trading port. It is a tortuous place for a fishing craft to negotiate, let alone schooners and ketches of considerable tonnage.'

A first pier was built in 1547 but soon broke up. Sir Richard Grenville's second pier of 1585 lasted better and was restored in 1740. Boscastle boats traded with Bristol, Gloucester and South Wales, taking out farm produce, tanning bark, slates and manganese ore from Launceston mines and bringing in groceries, coal, limestone and hardware. Today a small number of boats still fish there. The harbour is now in the hands of the National Trust, who ban cars from it for the benefit of its thousands of visitors.

The next port of consequence is Port Isaac (though Crackington Haven, Tintagel and Port William at Trebarwith, all fearsome accesses, handled ships during the nineteenth century). Attractively squeezed in between cliffs, it now fishes for mackerel and shellfish, to the delight of its many tourists. But in the last century Port Isaac had the largest pilchard fishery on the north coast after St Ives: the seining, bulking and packing employed most of the inhabitants. Forty-nine fishing vessels, with crews totalling 168, operated there in 1850. Two of the four 'penthouses' (curing cellars) are still evident, above the narrow beach on which cars now park at low tide. Around the corner at Port Gaverne, where there was never a quay, waggons of slates came down from Delabole, to be loaded into the holds of schooners beached there; chains of men and women handled the stones and packed them between layers of hay. When the railway arrived, Port Gaverne lost the trade.

Padstow is a port of great antiquity. By the time St Petroc arrived in the sixth century, there was a settlement using the same sort of

Port Isaac

hide-covered elongated coracles as the Mesolithic and Bronze Age people had used. The first stone pier was built in 1536, but before that Padstow ships sailed far and wide. In a fourteenth-century maritime lawsuit the *Mary* of Padstow was said to have been commissioned to sail to Bordeaux, to load wine there. In Tudor times the port traded with Wales, Ireland and the Severn ports and was a post town for Ireland. Ships were provisioned there for Elizabeth I's Irish campaign.

As the only good haven between St Ives and Bideford, Padstow's position ensured the growth of its seaborne commerce. By the late eighteenth century its ships were sailing to the Baltic and Russia, bringing back tallow, hemp and timber for shipbuilding. Six shipyards were operating there in the mid-nineteenth century, building schooners and ketches of up to eight hundred tons; the quarries on the Camel were still active, sending slates to Bristol, Ireland and South Wales.

The dreaded Doom or Dun Bar has always been the curse of Padstow: over three hundred wrecks occurred at the mouth of the Camel between 1760 and 1920, despite the valiant efforts of lifeboat crews, the provision of capstans to haul ships in, and the quarrying away of Stepper Point to reduce wind force. The advent of steam power overcame this. The Padstow lifeboat, previously often stranded by low tides, is now housed in a modern station at Trevose Head.

The shipyards closed with the passing of sail, but a brief prosperity came with the arrival of the London & South-Western Railway in 1899: an immense new fish dock brought hundreds of East Anglian and Scottish trawlers there during winter, and their catches were sent to Billingsgate by fish trains running direct from Padstow to Waterloo. Today the town is concerned mainly with tourism, which considerably threatens its age-old character, but recent harbour improvements have brought back visiting trawlers, and an efficient local fleet operates there. In summer the wide estuary is crowded at high tide with sailing craft of all kinds, from sail-boarders to large visiting yachts.

Today Newquay is the Brighton or Margate of Cornwall, but it has a Tudor quay from which local fishermen work and which berths the occasional yacht. The old Cornish name, Porth Lystry, means Boat Beach. The name New Quay was first recorded in 1439; an Indulgence issued by Bishop Lacey contributed funds to its repairs. In medieval times the Gannel estuary and Porth were the main ports, but both were unusable in heavy seas; then the haven was required, and the New Quay built under high cliffs was a safe anchorage in westerly gales.

Padstow: the inner harbour

The pilchard fishery of the nineteenth century brought a great expansion; soon a fleet of forty seining boats was bringing ashore huge hauls. The curing cellars have now disappeared, but the huer's hut, from which those massive shoals were spotted, is still preserved on the cliff above. J. T. Treffry acquired the harbour in the 1840s and brought copper there for export to the smelters in South Wales; later china clay went out by the same route.

On the Gannel foreshore, meanwhile, sailing schooners were being built; some 150 ships were owned at Newquay during this boom in coastal trade, which has left so little trace behind it. Before the railway had reached into Cornwall, tremendous trade was done in exporting local minerals and farm produce. Newquay's maritime trade ended when the GWR reached the town, but by then hotels and boarding-houses were mushrooming along the cliffs above the magnificent beaches, and another era was at hand.

Portreath, a few miles north of Redruth, is now entirely a tourist resort, but the harbour with its high granite quays and lock wedged between high cliffs, owned by Fox & Company, was shipping out a hundred thousand tons of copper for each year up to about 1850 and importing huge quantities of Welsh steam coal for the mining engines. About seven hundred ships berthed there each year, some twelve or thirteen per week: a measure of the immense industry of the mining boom.

Hayle is still a working port, though even more sand-bound than Padstow. It was the main exporter of copper in the great age (roughly 1760 to 1840) when Cornwall was known as 'the Copper Kingdom'. The rivalry between John Edwards, at Copperhouse to the east of the town, and John Harvey, on the western quays, resulted in the present port works. Edwards constructed the canal to bring ships to his foundry and smelting works.

Copperhouse ceased smelting in 1806; it was thenceforth more economical to take the ore to the coal in Wales than vice versa. The foundry supplied Cornish mines with engines and equipment until 1867. Meanwhile Harvey's foundry was employing over a thousand men; its winding gear, ore-crushing machines, pumps and steam-engines became world famous. Several Harvey engines were made for the Dutch government to drain the Haarlem Meer. Later Harvey's built iron ships and from 1830 ran a weekly packet service from Hayle to Bristol, calling at Padstow and Bideford. Besides passengers, broccoli, early potatoes, fruit and fish were carried and trans-shipped at Bristol for Cardiff or sent by railway to London, Birmingham and Manchester. The packet service ceased when the main railway line reached Hayle later in the nineteenth century.

Lelant, the mother village and churchtown of St Ives, was silted up by 1377. From then on St Ives flourished, sending its fish by pack-mules to markets at Marazion and Penzance. The first stone pier there was built in 1481, and the Borough took over the port from the Duchy of Cornwall, levying its own tolls. In 1770 John Smeaton, of Eddystone fame, designed the present pier; prior to the development of Hayle, St Ives was the main outlet for Penwith copper ore to Wales and Bristol. In 1835 some £1,800 in dues was collected there, a handsome sum in those times. Trade expanded with France, Ireland, Liverpool and London, and during the great days of pilchard seining (1830–50) an average of 22 million pilchards were caught there each year and exported to Italy direct.

Over five hundred people were then employed in the fisheries; decline followed, though by 1909 some two hundred vessels still

Newquay Harbour

sailed from St Ives, mainly for herring driving. The Hain Steamship Company had a fleet of sailing ships based there, trading across Europe and with the Americas. The diary of Captain John Tregerthen Short (1817–72) gives us an intimate picture of life in the heyday of the port. For instance (about 1828):

'A smuggler with 99 tubs of spirits and a crew of 6 men captured by the Preventive boat of St. Ives.'

'Capt. Moses Martin of the Preventive Service with the assistance of the pilot gigs and their crews took a smuggler with 339 tubs of spirits and a crew of 8.'

Evidence of the effectiveness of the campaign against smuggling after the Napoleonic Wars. An entry in 1829 concerns 'Schooner Eldred, 3rd vessel launched in 12 months set afloat in good style; some hundreds assembled on the beach.' Like Padstow, Newquay,

Par and many other Cornish ports, St Ives knew how to build good, seaworthy ships. But there were the ravages of the sea to be contended with: one entry in 1825 recorded, 'Nov. 10. Wind N.E.: very heavy gale, tremendous seas. Damage to shipping trivial, but some houses on the beach unroofed . . . the sea broke into the Churchyard, levelling graves and headstones.'

Artists discovered St Ives about 1890 and tourists followed with the railway but around its quayside the town, though improved, remains essentially an old-time fishing port. All the stink of fish has gone, no blood and guts run on the quays; but, as John Betjeman said, art has here triumphed over genteelism, and the little courts of cobbled streets of cottages are still there for us to enjoy.

The name Mousehole, pronounced 'Mouz'l', which has amused and baffled so many, probably comes from the medieval English

St Ives Harbour

maew, gull, and *holh*, basin: thus, Gull's Hollow. The old Cornish name Porth Enys (Landing Place with the Island) was a better description: St Clement's Island is outside the harbour, and a hermit manned a light there in the Middle Ages.

Fishing went on at the port before 1202, when the Bayonne merchants obtained curing rights there. Taking pilgrims to Santiago and Bordeaux (for Rome and the Holy Land) was a staple activity. Salted pilchards for Cornish families during the winter, and a growing trade to Catholic countries, brought prosperity. Although overshadowed later by Newlyn and Penzance, in 1849 some four hundred fishermen were sailing from Mousehole; there were as many packers, forty-five curers and four coopers making barrels. In 1861 a new granite pier almost encircled the harbour; but a slow decline followed. Today only small pleasure boats work there, and tourists line the quays of this harmonious little town huddled under Paul Hill.

Newlyn – the New Stream – was fishing before 1337; the French and Spanish attacked it during the Hundred Years' War. An Indulgence of 1455 encouraged the building of its first small pier. By 1826 it had expanded greatly with the tremendous catches of pilchards and mackerel, and its boats fished off Ireland for winter herring. From July on, the huer's trumpet or cry was heard, and the seine nets brought in vast shoals. Newlyn suplied the London market, sending its catches to Portsmouth for trans-shipment; from 1841, when Bristol was connected to Paddington by rail, much of the fish went overland to Hayle, to be taken up by Harvey's Packet. The harbour and quays were greatly extended after Acts of Parliament passed in 1866 and 1873, and today Newlyn is the premier Cornish fishing port and market. Trawlers from Scotland, Brixham, France, Belgium and the east coast of England, as well as locally registered boats, use it; the large harbour is often crowded with them. It is a splendid sight, despite fears that smaller Cornish boats will lose their traditional fishing grounds to larger foreign craft, including purse-seiners with their small-mesh nets. This was the home of nineteenth-century artists known as the Newlyn School, though few artists paint there now. But the old fish cellars and long-rooms for making nets still exist, though used for other purposes.

Penzance is a relatively quiet port today but has long memories of international trading. In the fifteenth century its vessels sailed to Southampton to trans-ship hides, pilchards, oil and cured fish to the Mediterranean. They also engaged in the wine trade and took Cornish woollen cloth to Gascony. Imports and exports increased with the expansion of mining. Timber came in from the Baltic, steam coal from Wales; long trains of packmules and horses brought copper

A corner of St Ives

ore from St Just in the late eighteenth and early nineteenth centuries, taking back coal to the mines. At that time Penzance also shipped out nearly half the Cornish tin production.

Many schooners, luggers and ketches were built there in the nineteenth century, and the Borough built a new pier in 1845. But Newlyn began to dominate the fishing trade, and the decline of mining severely affected Penzance. In the 1950s a large part of the harbour was filled in to make a car-park, and tourism in the form of yachts and pleasure craft brings more activity than cargo vessels. But the MV *Scillonian* sails daily for St Mary's with passengers and supplies, and the Holman Dock regularly repairs visiting ships.

Both Marazion and St Michael's Mount were thriving ports from the tenth century, when the priory was founded on the Mount. Marghas Vean (Little Market) and Market Jew (*Yow*, Thursday) were small settlements, succeeded now by the coastwise sprawl of Marazion. Despite the building of a harbour on the lee of the Mount, most ships ran ashore on the mainland beaches to load and discharge goods and Santiago pilgrims. The Mount, however, did good business in the eighteenth century, exporting cured fish, copper and refined tin and bringing in coal.

Porthleven is a Victorian port with a clocktower on the pier – another artificial harbour, begun in 1816, which, despite the money spent on it, never really flourished. Harvey's of Hayle leased it in 1854 and built the breakwater and inner basin with flood-gates, but despite a modest coastal trade it remained principally a fishing and boatbuilding port, which it is today.

Mullion Cove, today one of the pearls of the National Trust in Cornwall, has had a working past: it seined for pilchards in the eighteenth century but, having no cellars, its fish were taken to Newlyn. Later shellfish predominated, sent to Southampton by packet steamer calling from the Scillies. During the later nineteenth century pleasure steamers put in there in fine weather, to show their passengers the majestic cliff scenery and rocky islets. A few tripping and local fishing boats work from it today.

During the nineteenth century coasting vessels used Lizard Cove, a hazardous undertaking, but Coverack, on the east side of the Meneage peninsula, is the next real port. It was busy with fish in the thirteenth century and later served St Keverne parish with imports and exports, as well as supplying pilchard manure. Its pier of local serpentine stone was built in 1724. Porthallow and Porthoustock are tiny fishing ports; the latter has piers from which crushed stone from the quarry above was loaded until recently. Cadgwith, set in an idyllic gap in the cliffs, is now a holiday and tourist village, but its lifeboat station, which closed in 1960, has saved almost four hundred lives over the previous hundred years.

Gillan and Helford, once busy ports, are now quiet backwaters, but behind Pendennis Point is Falmouth, the largest port in Cornwall. The first real settlement there was promoted by the enterprising and piratical Killigrew family, who built Arwenack House in the sixteenth century. The hamlet, then known as Smithwick, grew up near it; the quay and custom house were built, and in 1661 the

Custom House Quay, Falmouth

borough of Falmouth was incorporated. Its real prosperity began in 1688, when it became a Post Office packet station.

The packets were small, speedy brigantines hired from local merchants or partnerships to take the mails, at first to Corunna and Lisbon, then to the West Indies and North American colonies; after 1706 the services were extended to Nova Scotia, Mexico, Brazil and Argentina. By 1827 some forty packets were running from Falmouth. They were armed, for during the later eighteenth and early nineteenth centuries they had to contend with French men o' war, with French, Spanish and American privateers and with Algerian pirates. In three years during the Napoleonic Wars, 1812–14, they fought thirty-two actions, from seventeen of which they emerged as victors, usually against superior firepower, though their losses were also heavy. They fought only if attacked: if it was impossible to escape or overcome the enemy, they had to sink their mails and surrender.

The packet crews traded on their own accounts, often smuggling cigars, port wine and brandy, transferring them to fishing vessels offshore and bringing them ashore at night. Falmouth flourished best in wartime, when naval ships assembled in the harbour to be provisioned and when prize cargoes were sold off. Sloops and brigs were stationed there to guard shipping entering the Channel.

The port lost the packet service to Southampton in 1852, but fishing was then booming and the great pilchard hauls came Falmouth's way: chandlering and victualling continued strongly, and ocean-going tugs were berthed there. A remarkable spate of shipbuilding in the creeks of the Haven produced scores of schooners and luggers, some of which opened up the fresh fruit trade with Spain. Four thousand ships used Falmouth in 1872; less than half of them were British. In 1912 there were 192 fishing craft registered there.

The railway reached Falmouth in 1863, and soon hotels grew up to accommodate the middle classes who came to enjoy the balmy sea air. Today Falmouth is a combined holiday resort, fishing port and ship-repairing centre: the successful dry dock there handles vessels of up to 85,000 tons. A proposal to create a container port there could bring a further injection of prosperity.

Norden described Penryn as 'A pretie market towne situate on the heade of a creeke of Falmouth Haven: it is a borrow towne governed by a Portreeve; it is a libertie of the Bishop of Exeter . . . at the end of the towne [is] the Abbey of Glasney, signyfing Green Water: and in these parts the Bishop hath good revenues and fayre woods.' The port was promoted by the bishops, and it soon took trade from Truro, farther up river; despite Falmouth's growth, it continued its seaborne trade until comparatively recently. In addition to fishing, there were exports of woollen cloth woven by a local mill, and of granite from Mabe and Carnsew. During the nineteenth century flour, paper and manure were made there, and coasting vessels were built.

Penryn was attacked by both the French and Spanish during Tudor times; Bishop Stafford built stone walls with stakes and chains as defences against them. At Glasney College the learned monks taught and wrote, leaving us the invaluable *Ordinalia* cycle of plays in Cornish. Today Penryn is a pleasant and quiet town set behind the main road, containing well-preserved Georgian and Victorian houses and a town hall with clock dividing its main street. Glasney has disappeared, though its foundations are still there, under some threat from developers.

The small ports of the Roseland, St Mawes, Porthscatho and

Portloe, and also Gorran Haven and Portmellon near Mevagissey, all flourished in the eighteenth and nineteenth centuries due to fishing. St Mawes provided services for its Tudor castle from 1530 on, and later pilots for Falmouth Haven were based there. Gorran was seining for pilchards before 1270 and exporting them to France. Today these are all primarily holiday resorts, but some fishing is still conducted from each of them.

Mevagissey had a pier in the fifteenth century, built by the local lord of the manor. Its great days began in the eighteenth century when the huge increase of seining, cellaring and exporting pilchards occurred. Stores and cellars were adapting from existing houses, but so narrow were the streets that not even pack animals could get through, and men and women carried the fish in panniers through them for distribution inland. A new pier was built in 1775, when the village was exporting 35 million pilchards each year.

After a depression during the French Wars the fisheries again expanded; by 1850 there were eighty boats operating, employing three hundred fishermen, packers and bulkers. The present pier (1866–70) tripled the size of the harbour. Today fishing continues, though not for pilchards, amid teeming tourists crowding the narrow alleyways; there is still a distinctively Cornish charm about Mevagissey, despite some ugly and brash commercial developments around the quays.

Both Charlestown and Par Harbours were specifically constructed to serve the industrial age of the late eighteenth century. Their promoters were brilliant and ruthless men possessing the will and the capital to achieve them. Charles Rashleigh, squire and mining adventurer, saw Polgooth mine and the infant china clay industry being served by ships beaching on the foreshore, a dangerous and time-consuming process. He employed John Smeaton to design a new harbour with lock gates for West Polmear cove; it was built during 1791–1805 and soon had ropemaking, shipbuilding and fish-bulking facilities, limekilns and a brickworks.

By 1850 the port, renamed Charlestown after Rashleigh, was shipping out a great deal of copper ore, fifteen thousand waggon loads of clay a year, and was importing all the coal and timber it could handle. From 1827 a huge forge worked there. Charlestown ships traded with Scandinavia, St Petersburg and the western Continent of Europe. Today the port is too small for the main clay trade, though coasters still load there, and summer visitors enjoy the Georgian calm of its houses and cottages and walk its granite quays.

Par is a proposition on a much vaster scale. Here the genius of J. T. Treffry, 'the King of Mid-Cornwall', reached its height: he enclosed thirty-five acres of water with a breakwater twelve hundred feet long,

Charlestown

and it took from 1829 to 1841 to complete. Par exported copper ore from his Fowey and Par Consols mines, and granite from his quarries at Luxulyan. The port built its share of schooners, which took china clay to the Mediterranean, the Baltic and South America. Today Par and Fowey are the chief sea outlets for kaolin. A complex of storage tanks, mineral grinding and drying plants, a railway waggon repair shop, coalyards and offices lies behind the harbour. The village of Par spreads around the bay beyond, its beaches providing caravan and camping sites; holiday-makers swim near the never-idle port, which handles about fourteen hundred ships each year.

Scant justice can be done here to a port with as long and eventful a history as Fowey's. Its importance as a trading link goes back at least to the Bronze Age, the Fowey estuary being an important harbour on the Ireland–Camel–France route. But before Domesday there was only a fishing hamlet on the present town site. Lostwithiel was the medieval commercial port, until the prior of Tywardreath granted Fowey its first charter in 1190.

With other south-western ports, Fowey was called on to supply ships for the King's Navy, to protect English domains in Bordeaux, Gascony and Brittany; it sent 47 ships and 770 men to the Siege of Calais in 1347, a total which must have meant scouring Lostwithiel and the country around. Fowey had much trouble from marauding French and Algerian pirates: the town was burned in 1380 and again in 1467, when Mrs Treffry of Place 'with her men repelled the French out of her house in her Housebonde's absence' (Leland).

The intrepid Gallants of Fowey, as they were known, soon turned to piracy themselves, flouting the laws of English monarchs. They had a chain across their harbour, but it was taken away by Edward IV and given to Dartmouth because, says Norden, 'They cut off the ears of the King's persuante; but they bowghte his eares with the confiscation and losse of some of their goodes and lives.'

In the early fifteenth century piracy was big business in Fowey. Mark Mixtow with his three ships, John Mixtow, who captured a Genoese caraval and brought back her rich cargo to sell off, and Hankyn Seelander, commissioned by the Crown to suppress pirates but seizing ships himself, all cocked their snooks at an unenforceable law. Soon the local merchants, squires and officials of Fowey and the district took part. John Willcocks in the *Barbara* seized fifteen ships off the Brittany coast inside a fortnight in May 1469. The Wars of the Roses were in progress, and Fowey men plundered with impunity.

But Henry Tudor (Henry VII) stopped all that, and Fowey turned to legitimate trade with Flanders, Brittany and Ireland. In 1530 St Catherine's Castle and the blockhouses were constructed, bringing a military presence there. Fishing grew over the next two centuries to such an extent that Dr Maton, visiting it in 1795, complained of 'the effluvia of salted pilchards' rising from the town and the fields thereabouts, where rotten fish was ploughed in for manure.

By the time the pilchard industry declined in the late nineteenth century, Fowey had become the main deepwater port for the china-clay schooners and steam vessels. Jetties were built above the town; today ships of up to ten thousand tons load there for destinations including North America, Australia and the Baltic. A good deal of yachting goes on in the non-tidal river mouth.

In 1549 Leland noted that to the east of Fowey was 'Poul Pier, a simple and poor village (a little fischar towne)'; but Polperro is older than that, appearing as Porthpirie in 1303 – Pirie's Landing place. Carew wrote of its fish jowters or jousters, men and women carrying large baskets of fish on their backs, selling around the countryside – something which went on into the later nineteenth century in west

Fowey

Cornwall. Polperro's almost landlocked harbour below perpendicular cliffs provides a fairly safe haven, though it has had its troubles. Thirty vessels were destroyed there by storm in 1817, and the pier was severely damaged by violent seas in 1774, 1817 and 1834. In 1976 a cloudburst swept down the narrow valley and through the village, causing devastation. Today, although fishing goes on with a small fleet of boats, Polperro derives greater trade from the thousands of visitors it receives annually.

Smuggling activities along the coast here grew enormously between 1770 and 1820. Arthur H. Norway, the late Victorian author of books on Cornwall, wrote, 'All joined in it; the smith left his forge, the husbandman his plough; even women and children turned out to assist in the unlawful traffic . . . Lusty seamen these, bearing no malice even when the revenue men scored a point', and went on to insist that this was all a natural extension of their fight to survive. Today a far more insidious and inexcusable form of smuggling goes on: heroin and other drugs are brought in too freely from yachts along the open coast of Cornwall, which is sadly depleted of coastguards and Customs officers.

The name Looe derives from *logh*, pool or lake (compare the Scottish *loch*, and Loe Pool near Helston). The twin boroughs of East and West Looe shipped streamed tin from Caradon from the late thirteenth century, and between them sent 315 men with twenty ships to the Siege of Calais. They declined with the rise of Plymouth and Fowey but went on importing iron, wine and canvas and sending out corn and fish. The canal from Moorswater revived their fortunes, and the quays were improved and a pier was built. When the railway was brought down from Caradon, granite and copper ore were loaded direct from trucks into ships. The trucks came of their own momentum down the long slope, controlled only by a brakesman, and horses pulled them back up again. A great deal of granite, however, was dressed on the quays for port works at Plymouth, Spithead, Portsmouth, Dover and elsewhere.

The pilchard fishery fed the local populace and added from time to time to their incomes. In 1853 the new bridge was built, and in the present century the boroughs were amalgamated under one town council. A small modern fishing fleet works there, but the quays serve mainly as car-parks for the many visitors who come there in summer to cram the narrow streets and sprawl out on the beaches.

Portwrinkle is an almost forgotten harbour, seventeen miles east of Looe on Whitsand Bay: here great pilchard harvests were brought ashore in the last century; the disused and all but ruined fish cellars are still standing. Cawsand and Kingsand, on the east of Rame Head, are no longer ports, but in Nelson's time they thrived by victualling the British fleet riding outside; they often accommodated its officers, including the admiral himself – who passed the night there with Lady Hamilton on several occasions.

Neither does Torpoint, on the Hamoaze, today rate as a port. Built in the eighteenth century as a result of the ferry service to Devonport,

Polperro

it acquired some attractive villas and Georgian houses; the establishment of the steam ferry on chains in 1834 brought more passing trade. Steam tugs worked from Torpoint to bring large vessels in and out of Plymouth docks. The car ferry (now diesel-powered) is today still a vital link for this spur of south-east Cornwall with the outside world.

Saltash, the last or first port in Cornwall, has had a long and illuminating history. Its Cornish name Essa, meaning Salt Water, is immemorial. Essa seafarers traded in medieval times with tin from

Dartmoor and Bodmin Moor; the place remained a flourishing seaport despite the rise of Plymouth opposite, and held its own maritime courts, which actually survived in an archaic form until the nineteenth century. The ferry passage to Devon has always brought trade.

Saltash ships ranged across the northern hemisphere: to Gascony and Ireland with troops, to Santiago with pilgrims and to Newfoundland for cod; one reached Finmark in 1483. During Elizabethan times its seamen served under Drake, Hawkins and Raleigh and fought against the Armada. The town was certainly prosperous in Norden's time, taking dues from the many craft anchored there. In 1584 he reported that 'the great Carrick that Sir Francis Drake browghte home so rich arrived here, and was here disburdened, and after fatally fyred'.

But Saltash soon found that Plymouth was taking more and more of her trade, and in 1724 Defoe called it a 'little, poor, shattered town . . . the ruin of a larger place'. Yet the market was still busy, its goods cheaper than those in Plymouth, and Saltash oysters were popular, being often sent up to Launceston for the delectation of the Assize judges. The mining age brought a revival: the port served the Cornish hinterland, along with other Tamarside quays farther up river, bringing in limestone, coal and timber and exporting market-garden produce, refined tin, copper ore and loads of granite. The building of Brunel's great railway bridge in the 1850s also increased prosperity. But today Saltash station is little used, as the townspeople drive their cars into Plymouth.

Saltash's rise, decline, revival and present near-extinction are very typical of the oscillating fortunes of so many Cornish ports; but the sea is always with us, and in one way or another Cornishmen will always earn their living from it.

5 Visitors' Cornwall

The true tourist, it ought not to need stating, is one who tours – that is, travels through new lands to enjoy their scenery and life. Many thousands of people come to Cornwall each year to holiday, and most of them do some touring, if only spasmodically and misguidedly. But the true tourist has come among us from time to time since John Leland, who rode through on horseback in 1538, writing his *Itinerary* of the kingdom for Henry VIII. Leland had a feeling for history as well as an eye for geography. 'St Burian,' he informs us, 'an Holy Woman of Ireland, sumtyme dwellid in this place, and there made an Oratorie. King Athelstan goying there, as it is sayde, and returning, made *ex vote* a College wher the Oratorie was.' (Athelstan established the College of Canons as a thanksgiving for his conquest of the Scillies.) Leland also described the great days of Fowey, thus: 'The Glorie of Fawey rose by the Warres in King Edward the first and third and Henry the v. Day, partely by Feates of Warre, partely by Pyracie, and so waxing rich felle al to Marchaundice; so that the town was hauntid with Shippes of diverse Nations, and their Shippes went to al Nations.'

Celia Fiennes was the first of that intrepid breed of British women travellers who have since, it seems, gone everywhere; she came to Cornwall in 1698 or 1699, riding side-saddle. Her diary is invaluable, endearing her to us with pithy and humorous comments. She was never sure where she would spend the next night, though the gentry often bedded and boarded her and her companions. At a St Austell inn she found men, women and children all smoking pipes, 'which was not delightful to me', but she enjoyed her first 'Westcountry Tart', an apple pie with custard and clotted cream.

She was fascinated by the tin-mines and found twenty, all viewed together, west of St Austell. She coveted the small Cornish horses (which she called Canelys – i.e. Goonhillies) for 'they are well made and strong and will trip along as light as on the stony road without injury to themselves, whereas my horses went so heavy that they wore their shoes immediately thin and off'. Penzance was short of fuel, since coal had to be brought round Land's End, braving privateers, so she had meat and broth there boiled on a fire of furze. She praised Launceston, with its castle 'which looks very great and in good repair . . . The whole town is of old houses of timber work'.

Daniel Defoe, not always a trustworthy witness, toured the Duchy in 1724. He liked Looe with its 'very beautiful and stately stone bridge' but thought it scandalous that the West and East boroughs sent two MPs each to Parliament, which 'is as much as the City of London chooses'. He was impressed by Falmouth: 'Ships of the greatest burthen come up to the quays, and the whole Royal Navy might safely ride in the Road.' Truro, however, was sadly declining as a port. Penzance had 'a good trade and a great many ships belonging to it', and he marvelled at the rich veins of copper, lead and tin he saw. Padstow was engaged mainly in the Irish trade, but contrary winds could make the voyage to Cork as long as six days.

Dr Richard Pococke travelled through Cornwall in 1750. He noted that St Austell was 'a little tinning town' with some granite houses and that Truro was doing very well from tin. He saw women and children 'breaking the country [earth] from the ore' and watched the

Botallack Tin Mine

stamping mills crushing it. At Redruth there was a 'great market of provisions weekly, attend by four or five thousand people': it was the place to buy shoes. He admired the newly built castle perched on boulders upon Carn Brea, but the 'disagreeable heaths' of West Penwith beyond St Ives were not to his taste – the romantic view of nature had not yet arrived. The Reverend William Borlase showed him his finds, and he inspected various antiquities like the Nine Maidens. Then to St Michael's Mount, the rich St Agnes tin-mines, Roche Rock with its hermitage reached by a precarious ladder – 'even some ladies of masculine courage have gone up into it' – and Pencarrow House near Wadebridge, with its Iron Age camp. Bodmin, full of ecclesiastical antiquities, was 'a long town, but seems very poor'. Then Restormel Castle and Lostwithiel, Liskeard, the Hurlers and Cheesewring rock-pile, and finally Calstock, which handled tin and made Cornish cloam ovens. A lively and precisely described tour.

The Reverend S. S. Shaw, coming through in 1788, was able to use a coach on the new turnpike roads. He saw, among many other things, a mayor-making ceremony at Lostwithiel; the St Austell mines; Fox & Company's smelting houses near Truro, which used charcoal to produce grain tin; Restormel Castle, draped in ivy; and St Matthew's Fair at Liskeard, the town full of sheep and oxen.

Young Dr W. G. Maton (1794–6) was a botanist and geologist. He found St German's a 'miserable borough town', despite its venerable church and the house of Port Eliot. The Looes were thriving chiefly by pilchard fishing, 'a business not likely to recommend them to visitors'. Fowey also assaulted his nostrils; he wrote that in time of pilchard scarcity the fishermen's families lived on limpets. There was then a bounty paid on exports of fish of 8s.6d. per hogshead, and he estimated that in a good year Cornish ports earned at least £50,000 all told from their catches.

In Truro blocks of tin were lying in the streets awaiting coining; each weighed over three hundred pounds – too large for thieves to carry away undetected. A large blowing house nearby had two reverberatory furnaces and employed twenty men; he noted that it took six hours to smelt six hundredweight of tin ore, producing 350 pounds of metal. Falmouth amazed and delighted him; yet it had no Parliamentary representative. Then on to Mullion and Kynance, the serpentine rocks and *Erica vagens*, the Cornish heath; to Penzance, 'the Montpellier of England', and the Wherry Mine, a wonder worked out in the sea itself, the miners going out in boats; it was drained by a pumping engine on shore, working a rod 240 yards long.

The Land's End he described in purple prose, but St Just he found 'a sad and dismall place in a cheerless corner of the country'. Then via

The Cheesewring

Chûn Castle to St Ives, its harbour chocked by sand, the stench of pilchards intolerable. Everyone there took part in the seining and packing operations, even deserting the church on Sundays if the fish appeared.

Crossing the notorious sands of the estuary to Hayle, Maton visited Harvey's foundry and Edward's smelter and went on to the Camborne mines. Dolcoath had reached a depth of 174 fathoms; Cook's kitchen, he recorded, employed 340 persons and had raised

Hayle

more than 300 tons of ore in one month. Then on, via St Columb, Bodmin and Wadebridge to Tintagel, where he suspected that the castle was not so antique as to be early British. There he saw Cornish choughs flying over the cliffs and found tame ones kept in gardens. Bossiney, a mere few cottages without even an inn, had six voters electing two MPs. He was unsure of his reaction to the country and the cliffs – sometimes they were 'bleak and rugged', but Boscastle he thought was in a highly romantic situation, with 'fine mountainous eminences about the village and harbour'. Thence he went to Launceston, 'populous and extensive . . . altogether very respectable', to Callington, briskly manufacturing cloth, and the Cheesewring, 'constructed by Nature in one of her whimsical moments'.

Dr Maton was one of the last horseback travellers. A different attitude was adopted when Wilkie Collins came on his walking tours in 1850. He and an artist companion produced *Rambles Beyond Railways: Notes taken in Cornwall A-foot*. Collins certainly contributed to a new interest in the Duchy; the railway had reached Plymouth and by the time the book was reprinted had extended into Cornwall via the Tamar Bridge; a whole new public could now contemplate coming west and following Collins' ramblings.

At Looe, 'one of the prettiest and most primitive places', the pair were fascinated by the flower-filled gardens crowded together on steep terraced slopes, by the medieval bridge, the clear light, the changing sea, the 'pell-mell shops selling gingerbread, shirts, studs, and two-and-ninepenny hats' among much else. They witnessed a regatta and a 'great tea-drinking' along with the entire populace. Indeed, the Cornish politely welcomed them, with some curiosity it is true. Collins soon realized that here was a race apart – 'National feeling is almost entirely merged in the local feeling; a man speaks of himself as Cornish in much the same spirit as a Welshman speaks of himself as Welsh.'

At Fowey, also full of flags and conviviality on Regatta Day, they were stared at as they went about with their knapsacks. That anyone should choose to walk through the country rather than ride was inconceivable; they were often taken for pedlars or 'trodgers', and some offered to buy tea from them. Collins was not impressed by Helston, but their object was to get to the Lizard and other natural wonders nearby. They had their share of 'Cornish weather' – being told that the fine drizzle could last a fortnight. But they saw the Lizard and Kynance on fine days, and they are described lovingly and dramatically. Victorian England loved the pen-picture and came to see for itself.

A whole chapter on the pilchard fisheries is one of the most valuable accounts we have; Collins was enraptured at the great catches – 'one teeming, convulsed mass of shining, glancing, silvery scales: one compact crowd of tens of thousands of fish, each one of which is madly endeavouring to escape, appears in an instant'. It all gave 'active employment to a hardy and honest race who would starve without it'.

After seeing Land's End they went to Botallack Mine, then one of the memorable experiences Cornwall had to offer: the Queen and Consort had visited it in 1846, and the Prince and Princess of Wales came there in 1865. Out under the sea into the dark galleries, hearing the 'low, mysterious murmur of the sea above' they went, having descended by means of terrifying landings and structures set in the cliff face.

Moving back up the coast, they visited Piran Round, where (having got hold of a copy of the Creation play) Collins visualized a medieval performance of the Cornish Mystery. To the Carmelite convent of St Mawgan in Lanherne, then to Tintagel: more vivid descriptions, of the ruined castle on the precipitous cliffs, and speculations on Arthur and his knights. St Knighton's (Nectan's) Glen and the legend of the Forrabury Bells; then to Launceston and a 'return to England'. The book is a joy to read even today.

A spate of accounts of walking tours followed, appearing as books

Gurnard's Head

and in the national Press over the next forty years. Walter White's *A Londoner's Walk to the Land's End*, J. T. Blight's *A Week at the Land's End* and Mrs Craik's *Tour of Cornwall* in 1884 were some of the best. But the true guide-book, in the shape of *Murray's Handbook for Tourists in Devon and Cornwall* (1851) was already being written when Collins undertook his Rambles. It was the first of many and the most comprehensive of all, surveying geology, antiquities, fishing, mining, the 'Old Language' and the Duchy of Cornwall, as well as providing many detailed itineraries. Murray's visitors would arrive by train at Plymouth or by packet boat at Falmouth or Mevagissey, then take coaches. Perusing the book, we are back in another world, but considerable efforts were already being made to cater for tourists.

Bude Haven: (inn, the Falcon): 'a small watering place on a grand and curious coast'. Sea bathing described. The canal is active; among

Tintagel Castle

excursions, Moorwinstow (Morwenstow) is recommanded for its impressive scenery and splendid Anglo-Norman church.

Boscastle: one mean public house. The setting is praised; the narrow harbour 'admits two or three vessels at a time'. Many magnificent walks in the vicinity are recommended and local legends told, as well as the history of the Bottreaux family.

Tintagel Castle, its supposed Arthurian associations and the remains of a landing stage under it, are described. There is one inn at Trevena village. Delabole Quarry is given full treatment; it employs twelve hundred men and provided 120 tons of best-quality slate a day. Port Isaac is not mentioned. Padstow (two inns) is 'one of those antiquated fishing towns which are viewed most agreeably from a distance'. But it has Prideaux Place, the splendid harbour and Doom Bar, among other sights.

Newquay in 1851 offers the Old Inn and the Red Lion only: 'a small watering place where the pilchard fishery is pursued on a considerable scale'. The cliffs are described as romantic. The railway is imminent, being built from Par along Treffry's plans. Much geological interest in the coast. Perranzabuloe has an inn and 'is a small bathing place on a sandy cove'. An excursion from Truro, recommended for accommodation, is suggested. (Truro people had for some fifty years been going to Perranporth to bathe.) The newly exposed first church of St Piran and Piran Round are described. Otherwise this is a desolate place.

St Ives, however, is compared with a Greek village in the marvellous light of West Penwith, but it is still 'abominably tainted with the effluvia of fish cellars'. Tregenna House, built in 1774, and John Knill's pyramid are of interest, but there is no recommendation to stay there. Penzance is coming into its own, offering ample hotels and guesthouses and the manifold antiquities and scenery of the Land's End district. There are hot and cold sea baths, the newly built esplanade, the spring and summer plants blooming there in midwinter, the Wherry Mine and Botallack: so much to offer the well-to-do invalid and curious visitor.

Falmouth too is becoming tourist-conscious. There are the Royal and Greenbank Hotels to stay in; the town is expanding with 'handsome and commodious dwellings'. The Royal Cornwall Polytechnic Society (1833) is meeting to encourage science, art and industry. Exotic plants flourish in the gardens.

Newquay: view from the Bowling Club

The Fowey estuary: view from Polruan

Mevagissey offers nowhere to stay but the modest Ship Inn, and is noted for 'dirt and pilchards', but its magnificent setting invites a visit. Caerhayes Castle, Polgooth Mine and Bodrugan's Leap are suggested as excursions. Looe must have improved considerably, for in a lively and lush description there is no mention of smells, and pilchards are barely mentioned. Polperro, in an 'eminently romantic situation', is to be visited mainly for the fossils in its cliffs.

In 1880 Walter H. Tregellas produced his *Tourist's Guide to Cornwall*. The main railway line to Penzance has been opened, and there are significant developments following it. Tregellas' pride in his homeland is much apparent in his flowery style: his countrymen are 'ardent and vivacious, self-reliant and versatile', and their climate is most beneficial to all. One wonders whether he would have been quite so enthusiastic in promoting tourism if he could have foreseen today's scene.

In 1880 there are seventy lodging-houses at Bude and two inns. Bathers are warned of crumbling cliffs of 'contorted carboniferous strata'. The railway has reached Holsworthy, and coaches run there from Bude, and to Barnstaple and Launceston. Padstow still evidently holds no comforts for the visitor, but Tregellas praises its situation and comments on the marine activities. Newquay is a 'rising watering place' and a busy port and fishing station. Three hotels are recommended, and there are numerous lodging-houses; the Tea Caverns, in former smugglers' caves, are a feature to visit. There are some colourful descriptions of nearby cliff scenery, including Bedruthan Steps and Trevelgue Head.

Perranporth now offers 'homely accommodation'; the fine beach, St Piran's Oratory and Piran Round are still the main attractions. St Ives has been connected to the railway system since 1877; according to Tregellas it is 'an old, straggling, and not very inviting town (but improving), beautifully situated and at one time a favourite resort for the fashionable of Penwith'. The Great Western Railway has acquired Tregenna House and opened it as an hotel. A new drainage system and town reservoir have been constructed. Ladies bathe from tents on Porthminster Beach, men and boys from Penolver Rocks.

Penzance's mild climate is again praised, as 'highly beneficial to invalids suffering from chest or throat complaints'. Three hotels are listed, and the various excursions to Land's End, Mousehole and the antiquities itemized. Falmouth, connected by railway since 1867, continues to expand; St Mawes is now mentioned as a small, select resort.

Looe (two thousand inhabitants) still ships out granite and ore; the town is praised as an attraction, but only one inn is recommended.

The *Thorough Guide to North Devon and North Cornwall* (1890) outlines further developments. The railway network has been extended with branch lines from Gwinear Road to Helston, and Lostwithiel to Fowey. Bude is now described as a 'widely scattered and disjointed village, yearly increasing in size and popularity'. Boscastle is 'an unattractive village', the harbour and cliffs being its main assets. A bed for the night at the newly built Wellington Hotel cost 4s.6d, breakfast 2s.6d and dinner 3s.6d – somewhat high charges. Tintagel is hardly yet ready for a tourist invasion, though the Wharncliffe Hotel is now recommended. But the castle ruins are evidently attracting hundreds, the local vicar is now officially custodian of the castle (reviving an ancient Duchy office) and a cottage near the cliffs offers refreshments to those who undertake the arduous climb down and up.

Legs are still much in vogue as a means of travel: a walk of twenty-five strenuous miles along the cliffs to Padstow is suggested. Port Isaac is now mentioned (though rather tentatively); it offers a dingy inn or two. Lodgings are offered at Polzeath. Padstow is 'a mean looking place of woebegone aspect' with one inn to stay at, the Commercial. 'We imagine no one deliberately visits Padstow for its own sake, but those fond of a fine coast will find it a convenient resting place for the night.' Stepper Point and its seals, Trevose Lighthouse and Prideaux Place are the main attractions.

In 1890, this Guide tells us, there are several large hotels at Newquay; beds are 5 shillings a night at the Great Western, the latest of them. The arrival of the railway in 1875 has had an immense effect: the town is a mile-long street along the clifftop. China clay is being exported from the harbour, drainage has been installed and reservoir water is available. Excursions from Newquay are thriving: to Perranzabuloe, Cubert, Crantock, Bedruthan Steps, Roche Rock and the Luxulyan Valley – recommended as the most delectable inland trip, with views of the Treffry Viaduct, the tors and granite boulders, and the 'deep and sylvan glen', which, however, is thick and white with china clay washings.

Perranporth is growing; the Perranporth Hotel is recommended, but the place is still a small and straggling village. We are warned that bathing near the cliffs is dangerous. At St Ives the Tregenna Castle Hotel provides beds at 4s.6d per night; other hotels are listed. Fishing continues with a large fleet, but there is no mention of detractions. The town, expanding with 'pleasantly situated residences on the higher ground above the station, is a convenient base for exploring the Land's End district, by foot or coach'. St Ives Consols mine is still working; Botallack has closed, but Levant works can be visited. Penzance offers six hotels, three churches, public baths and omnibus services. There is a wide choice of lesser lodgings.

Padstow lifeboat being launched at Trevose Head

On the Scillies there is a hotel at St Mary's and one at Tresco.

By 1930 the picture has changed considerably. The railway network, complete since 1900, is bringing more and more visitors each summer, including the lower middle classes who stay in boarding-houses or bed-and-breakfast accommodation. The motor car brings down wealthier families who now are beginning to own their holiday homes around the coast. Ward Lock's Guide of 1930 finds Padstow 'a queer, busy little place, delightfully situated, now realising that it possesses every necessary qualification as a holiday resort'. Most of the bays around the coast have by now acquired some buildings, and a rash of uncontrolled inter-war development is well under way, threatening to despoil much of the glorious coast the visitors come to enjoy.

Port Isaac now rates a page or so, as a delightfully quaint and old-world spot. Villages like Cubert, Crantock and St Agnes have inns, cafés and tea gardens. Perranporth is developing fast, more or less as we know it today; James Braid laid out its golf course in 1928, and the walk to the Lost Church in its hideous concrete casing is marked out by white stones in the dunes. St Mawes is a gracious and exclusive small resort. St Ives has grown, but the old port area is still intact.

In 1947 Town and Country Planning became law; it inhibited the growth of sporadic development and thus saved most of the coves and bays of Cornwall from further despoilment, though it allowed a new type of holiday complex, often sited far too conspicuously: the caravan park. From 1960 to 1980 caravans proliferated, often congesting the minor roads and small towns, though the recession has since moderated their influx. The axeing of railway branch lines in the 1950s and 60s increased the emphasis on motor cars and necessitated large-scale road improvements. During recent years, between two and three million people have holidayed in Cornwall each year.

Though some hotels have gone out of business, most have survived

Treglos Hotel, Constantine Bay

the recession, due to package deals, winter breaks and the holding of functions out of season, such as dinners and conferences. Tourist parks, self-contained areas providing practically everything on site, are new ventures; some even have their own private beaches. Generally they affect the landscape less than other developments, being well screened by trees and off the main roads. Self-catering chalets, cottages and villages are the strongest trend in the mid-1980s.

Beach and harbour authorities, used to dealing with surfers, yachts and pleasure craft, are now faced with modern sports such as water ski-ing, hang-gliding, parascending and aqua-diving. Beach guards and rescue services, the latter often voluntary, have perforce been established to protect and save the unwary and thoughtless tourists who endanger themselves and others.

Cultural amenities, in the past few and poor, have dramatically altered, benefiting from the attendance of visitors as well as residents. Music festivals at St Germans, St Columb, St Endellion, Perranuthnoe and Truro (centred on the cathedral) bring national and international artistes to Cornwall, to perform with local choirs and ensembles. Professional drama is spasmodic and unpredictable,

Minack Theatre, Porthcurno

depending on Arts Council grants, but several travelling groups are at present taking their work around the towns and villages. At the Minack, a Greek-styled amphitheatre at Porthcurno, a hugely popular summer season of plays is put on each year. There was a revival of Cornish drama at Piran Round from 1969 to 1974, indelibly scoring its successes on the minds of theatre-goers; there are hopes of reviving this medieval tradition.

Art galleries are open throughout the Duchy; St Ives and West Penwith no longer dominate to the extent they used to. In fact, exhibiting and selling paintings, pottery and small *objets d'art* are now inextricably interwoven with the pattern of tourism in Cornwall.

The growth of small town and other museums must surely merit wholehearted approval; those at Bodmin, Camelford, Lostwithiel, Fowey, St Ives, St Mary's (Scilly) and Padstow, among others, present their deeply fascinating exhibitions of their pasts and are well supported by discerning visitors. Other museums offering compre-

Wheal Martyn China Clay Museum

hensive displays and accounts of past methods of working tin, clay and slate have been opened, with considerable capital outlay, at Wendron, Geevor, St Austell, Redruth and Delabole. Their exhibits and working machinery bring home in the most impressive way the problems our Cornish forebears faced in digging out the wealth of their rocks and subsoil in order to earn their bare living. In our relative prosperity, among all our modern conveniences and electronic gadgetry, they allow us sobering glimpses into the different world that is still not so very far behind us.

6 Traditions, Customs and Language

The unique features of the Cornish way of life have resulted largely from Cornwall's remoteness from the rest of Britain and to some extent from its links with other Celtic countries, especially Ireland, Wales and Brittany. Its language, now being successfully revived, is a sister tongue to those of the latter two.

The first Cornish custom of the year is Hurling, an ancient game played by any number of men against a rival team of like number, in which a silver ball (in the past, it is said, a golden one) is thrown or hurled. It is like a huge aerial game of rugby football, played over a whole parish, or even several parishes: for inter-parish Hurls were a feature of the past. St Columb v. St Mawgan, Camborne v. Redruth, St Ives v. Lelant, St Just v. St Buryan or Sancreed, and so on; in the seventeenth and eighteenth centuries these were great events, and often feelings between the opponents ran so high that injuries and sometimes even deaths resulted.

Hurling was mentioned by both Carew and Norden; Carew devoted three pages to the sport. In east Cornwall they played 'hurling to goal', the goals being two bushes set perhaps a mile apart. In the west they played 'hurling to country', the goals being two gentlemen's residences several miles apart. The ball, says this vivid historian, 'may be compared to an infernal spirit, for whosoever catcheth it fareth straightways like a madman, struggling and fighting with those to go about to hold him'. Carew is dubious as to the virtues of this boisterous and injurious game. The gentry seem to have adopted it, much as public schools later took to rugby: two great hurls were held in Hyde Park in the seventeenth century, one with Oliver Cromwell present. On both occasions the participants were guests of a Cornish gentleman being married in London. Carew confirms that hurlings were 'mostly used at weddings'.

That the sport began as a fertility rite seems likely. The two dates on which St Columb Major, now the only parish devoted to it with religious enthusiasm, holds its Hurls, have been thought to be associated with the ancient Celtic festival of Imbolc, which fell in February about the time of Shrove Tuesday – the nearest Christian

Hurling at St Columb Major

festival, to which it later became attached. Imbolc signalled the lactation of ewes and the dropping of the first lambs; it was thus the first harbinger of spring. The strengthening sun was represented by a golden ball which, also a male fertility symbol, was handled, thrown, wrestled and fought for. One of the early entries in the St Columb Green Book, a register of parish dealings, referred (in 1595) to a 'sylver ball gylt'.

Hurling continued strongly throughout Cornwall until the days of the Methodist revival, when it fell into disrepute. Polwhele (1803) wrote that like wrestling it was then confined 'to the inferior Classes'. By 1865 it was dying fast, though St Columb Major and St Columb Minor still played against each other on the beaches at Newquay. Today there is hurling for young people on the sands at St Ives on Bank Holidays, but the great occasion is on Shrove Tuesday and the Saturday week following it, when the windows of shops and houses at St Columb Major are boarded or wired up and the young men of the town play against those of the country parts of the parish. After the day's festivities the ball is ceremonially dipped in a brew at the Silver Ball Inn, and the hurlers quench their thirsts with 'Silver Ale'.

Many customs were, until the days of the Commonwealth and the ascendancy of the Puritans, common in one form or another all over Britain; they continued on the Continent and in Ireland, some down to the present day. In remoter Cornwall two of the most remarkable and famous have survived and are prospering: Padstow Obby Oss and the Helston Furry Dance.

Padstow's black-painted canvas monster, hardly any more a horse, snaps and swirls and cavorts all over his town, the undisputed Lord of *Cala Me*, the First of May. Led by his 'dancer' or 'teazer', enacting with him a kind of mimed duel with his painted club, he is followed by a party of men and girls in white, flower-bedecked, and a troupe of drummers and musicians playing their vigorous, haunting and unique May Song. It is a spectacle to lift the heart and set the blood beating faster, and thousands come to see it each year. Yet less than a century ago this was a degraded ceremony, scorned by historians and disparaged by the well-to-do. The folklore revival of the early twentieth century claimed attention for it, and it was reformed after the 1914–18 War, to expand and organize itself for today's great occasion.

The original Padstow hobby horse seems to have been quite small, a relative of the little Morris hobbies that attend or attended many folk customs. Morris dances and customs have their fertility associations, and Padstow's May Day and horse-mask certainly have theirs; the event must go back to the Celtic summer festival of Beltaine and probably before that, to the Bronze or Neolithic Age. The greenery brought into the town, the symbolic mating with young women abducted under the skirts of the Oss, and many lines in the age-old song, all create an atmosphere of procreation and rebirth. The Padstow Oss, bigger now than any hobby elsewhere, dances out to bring the summer in, to the delight of the townspeople, whose true and ancient religion one feels this is.

By contrast the Helston Furry Dance (Cornish *fer*, fair or feast) is now a sedate and formalized occasion. Yet it has many affinities with the Padstow custom, and the two must originally have been versions of the same Beltaine rites. Wilkie Collins heard no good of the Furry: 'A sort of barbarous carnival . . . even the "genteel" residents allow themselves to be infected with the general madness.' Properly revived by the Helston Old Cornwall Society in 1930, it is now a decorous but impressive event, the townspeople conducting themselves in formal attire, the ladies in flowing dresses and colourful hats, twirling in and out of the streets and through the very houses of the town. The Hal-an-two, a mummers' play about St Michael

Padstow: May Day

killing the dragon, is a delightful precursor to it all, acted round the streets by the young people.

For some centuries the origin of the main dance was confused with the cult of the Roman goddess Flora; the festivity has now reverted to its true Cornish name. But the great glory of the occasion is the grand stately tune, one without original written music, as played by the Helston Band; it is imitated all over Cornwall and outside but never surpassed. It has notes and phrases in common with the Padstow tune, though its rhythm is more ponderous.

Like the Padstow and Helston celebration, the Midsummer Eve bonfires, illuminating the country from Land's End to the Tamar, were originally Beltaine customs; during the Celtic era they took place on May Eve and were in honour of Bel or Belinus, the sun god. Cattle and sheep were driven between bonfires to purify them. After the coming of Christianity the event was moved to St John's Eve, 23 June; in west Cornwall St John's Eve fires went on, widely supported, until the First World War. Today, revived with a rather sober ceremony by the Federation of Old Cornwall Societies, the Lady of Flowers casts her bouquet into the fire as it is lit on the hilltop, chanting in Cornish an invocation that the weeds be destroyed and a thousand good seeds spring up.

On the Monday after 7 July, the Feast of Thomas à Becket, the festival of Bodmin Riding used to take place. From medieval times the Riding was part of the Feast Day and would be followed by a Janticle, i.e., sports and other celebrations. The significance of the date is said to be that on that day St Petroc's bones were restored to Bodmin Priory. The Riding was a ceremonial parade, led by all who could ride horses, and may originally have been a beating of the bounds ceremony to 'prove' the monastery lands around Bodmin. During the Middle Ages the gilds of the town with all their craftsmen took part; later, carriages and coaches were included. Garlanded, they paraded the town with a band playing the jaunty tune known as

Helston Furry Dance

the Bodmin Riding March, presented their garlands to the priory and then resorted to the sports and other celebrations.

Despite the frowning impact of Methodism and Bible Christianity, the custom went on until 1824 or 1825, with wrestling, bell-ringing and other sports over several days. In 1864 T. Quiller Couch wrote that it was 'hopelessly dead'; there were, however, two later attempts to revive it, one in 1930 by the town's Old Cornwall Society, and another by the Town Council in 1974 and 1975. With its joyous, insistent Riding March, it is now happily to be resurrected, to take its place alongside other venerable Cornish customs.

Cornish (or more properly Celtic) wrestling is a sport of great antiquity, now practised principally by the Cornish and Bretons, though a version of it has also survived in Cumbria, the land of the North Britons. The style uses only holds above the waist; the wrestlers wear short trunks and canvas jackets which can be gripped by their opponents. Previously this sport prevailed also in Devon (with variations).

The most famous match of all time was that between the Cornish champion James Polkinhorne of St Columb and Abraham Cann of Devon at Devonport, in 1826; both were heavyweights. Seven thousand spectators laid huge wagers on the match. Cann was favourite and wore specially hardened kicking shoes; Polkinhorne, barefoot, wore leather leggings. There was a dispute over the final verdict, but Polkinhorne undoubtedly lifted his man on high and dashed him to the ground to win the third 'fall'. A plaque to the Cornishman may be seen on the wall of the Red Lion Inn at St Columb, where he was landlord of a now defunct public house.

Other great wrestlers of their day were Thomas Gundry of Goldsithney in the eighteenth century, Parkin of St Columb Minor, who was fifty-three when Polkinhorne fought Cann, and the Chapman family of St Wenn, who produced a string of champions of various weights during the early to middle years of the present century. Today Cornish wrestling tournaments are a regular feature of Cornish life during the summer months, and since 1928 the Cornish Wrestling Association and its Breton counterpart have arranged numerous visits of Cornish teams to Brittany to wrestle against the Bretons, and to bring Breton teams to Cornwall for similar contests.

'Crying the Neck', an immemorial custom, has been revived with sporadic gatherings, mainly in west Cornwall. It harks back to the primitive times when harvesting parties would save the last swathe of corn, plaiting from it a corn dolly wherein, they believed, resided the spirit of the corn, to hang over the farmhouse hearth until the next

Cornish wrestling

harvest. In Cornwall the 'Neck' was severed by the last reaper and held up: he shouted 'I have 'en! I have 'en! I have 'en!.' The others would chorus, 'What 'ave 'ee?' What 'ave 'ee? What 'ave 'ee?' – 'A Neck! A Neck! A Neck!' – followed by cheering and the consumption of cider, beer and buns. Often a Neck Feast was held in the

'Crying the Neck': about 1930

farmhouse kitchen or outside. It was an echo of the oldest basic custom, the celebration of another year's vital sustenance gathered in, a thanksgiving to our earliest gods.

On the first Saturday of September the Gorseth of the Bards of Kernow meets at some historic site in Cornwall. It is an impressive modern ceremony marking Cornish culture and identity, a gathering of hundreds of blue-robed Bards, attended by thousands of spectators and the media. Modern it is, in this form, though it is evident that the Gorseths of the Old Britain met at various sites all over the isle, one of them being Boscawen Un circle near St Buryan, where the first Cornish Gorseth was held in 1928.

The bards of antiquity were Court poets and speakers for their princes; all over Europe they sang and declaimed their verses. The Welsh Gorsedd (*gorsedd, gorseth*: a meeting or session) was revived in 1792, and the Breton Gorseth during the nineteenth century; the first Cornish Grand Bard, Henry Jenner, had been admitted as Gwas Myghal (Servant of Michael) in Brittany. Today official bardic guests and sometimes Archdruids attend Gorseth Kernow from those sister Celtic lands.

The ceremony is entirely in Cornish, apart from the announcements of prize-winners of various competitions, for young and old are encouraged to write poems, essays and songs in Cornish, English and Cornish dialect. The songs sung during the Gorseth are fervent expressions of loyalty to Kernow, the Celtic land of Cornwall, and include '*Bro Goth Agan Tasow*', the Cornish version of 'Land of My Fathers', whose tune the Bretons also use:

Bro goth agan Tasow, dha fleghes a'th car,
Gwlas ker a'n howlsedhas, pan vro yu dha bar?
War oll an norvys, 'th on'ny scullyes a-les,
Mes agan kerensa yu dhys!
Old land of our fathers, thy children love thee,
Dear land of the sunset, what realm is your equal?
Over all the earth, we are scattered afar,
But our love is yours!

At the central point in the proceedings the seven-feet-long sword representing Excalibur is held aloft, and the Bards all swear fealty to Cornwall. Modern bards are admitted for services rendered to the Cornish homeland, artistic or social, and for proficiency in the revived Cornish language; a number of exiles from across the world are recognized for services to Cornish communities overseas.

The remarkable story of the decline, near extinction and present day revival of Cornish is one to inspire any believer in lost causes;

Gorseth Kernow: the Gorsedd of Cornwall

indeed, today this fact is a shining light to other Celtic peoples, whose languages are fighting grim rearguard actions against the massed battalions of mass-media and American–English phraseology.

Cornish – Kernewek – is a descendant of the ancient British (Brythonic) tongue, which was spoken over most of mainland Britain and Brittany until the advance of the Germanic people broke it up into what have since become Welsh, Cornish and Breton. Cornish has only a small though very significant body of literature, from which the present tongue has been resuscitated.

The principal surviving works are The Passion Poem, *Pascon Agan Arluth*, a long work of some poetic value; the three mystery plays known collectively as the *Ordinalia* (which actually means

Prompt-Book) and *Bewnans Meriasek*, the life of St Meriasek of Camborne, the only extant saint's play in Britain. These plays were performed and written down in the fourteenth and fifteenth centuries, the golden age of Cornish literature, the monks of Glasney College, Penryn, being almost certainly the scribes and organizers of the productions. A third play, *Gwryans an Bys*, The Creation of the World, has also come down to us; it is a sixteenth-century Renaissance version of the first *Ordinalia* play, *Origo Mundi*. Both Creation plays are vivid and highly dramatic portrayals of the scriptures and, with the Passion and Resurrection Plays, must have entranced the illiterate people who were exhorted to attend them at Corpus Christi, a general holiday in the later Middle Ages.

The plays were put on at places like Piran Round, Plain an Gwarry at Redruth, and certainly Penryn itself. Carew gives a somewhat satirical description of these 'Gwary Miracles' and their venues; they evidently survived until his times, after which Puritanism killed them off. 'The country folk flock from all sides, many miles off, to hear and see it, for they have therein devils and devices to delight as well the eye as the ear.' In their full flower these plays, with their cosmic, sweeping themes, must have been mighty and moving spectacles, as seen in their traditional venues, the open-air rounds of Cornwall. In performance, as we know from successful revivals in the 1960s and 70s, they compare very favourably with the various English cycles of Mystery plays.

After the failure of the 1549 Prayer Book Rebellion, English church services replaced those in Latin, though some sermons in Cornish were permitted (the last was at Landewednack in 1678), and the catechism was still conducted in Cornish, where it was the main language. But the imposition of Anglicanism was a mortal blow to Kernewek, and the increasing involvement of Cornwall in the trading and seafaring affairs of England soon meant that Cornish went out of use commercially and culturally. By the last decades of the eighteenth century only a few people in West Penwith spoke it; many Cornish-speakers would not teach it to their children, it being thought inferior. William Bodenor learned his Cornish from the Mousehole fishermen with whom he went to sea. Dolly Pentreath, the last monoglot Cornish-speaker (she refused to speak English), died in 1777 and has a memorial to her in the old tongue at Paul.

Yet the language was not dead, merely out of use. Many people 'treasured up the fragments' – the Lord's Prayer, the Ten Commandments, the numerals, some old sayings. There has survived the ancient *englyn* or triplet, a stirring reminder:

Scene from the *Ordinalia*, at Piran Round

An lavar coth yu lavar gwyr:
Byth dorn re ver dhe'n tavas re hyr;
Mes den hep tavas a gollas y dyr.
The old saying is a true saying:
Always a hand too short to a tongue too long;
But the man without a language lost his land.'

Tonkin in 1704 recorded a sharp proverbial view of marriage:

Kensa bledhen, byrl ha bay;
Nessa bledhen, lul ha lay;
Tressa bledhen, kemer ha dry;
Peswartha bledhen, mollath Dew war-ef a wruk dry agan deu warbarth!
First year, kiss and play;
Second year, lullaby; [i.e. children born]
Third year, fetch and bring;
Fourth year, the curse of God on him who brought us two together!

It was left to the antiquarians and linguists to lay the foundation of the revival which few could have believed would ever come. There was Edward Lhuyd's *Archaeologia Britannia*, which in 1707 compared Gaelic, Welsh and Cornish; Edwin Norris' publication, in Cornish and English, of *The Ancient Cornish Drama* (the *Ordinalia*) in 1858; Whitley Stokes' *Gwryans an Bys*, 1864, and *Bewnans Meriasek*, 1872 – the latter had lain in the library of Peniarth, thought to be an old Welsh text. The Reverend Robert William's *Lexicon Cornu-Britannicum*, a proto-dictionary, came in 1865; and 1901 saw Henry Jenner's *Handbook of the Cornish Language*, among much else.

Interest grew down to the common people after the First World War, and the foundation of Old Cornwall Societies in the 1920s generally encouraged interest. Robert Morton Nance, who was to succeed Jenner as Grand Bard, taught and wrote tirelessly over four decades, and his *Cornish Dictionaries* of 1936–8, in his unified spelling, provided the bones of the revival which, exploding in the 1970s, has created the Cornish Language Board and its associate Cowethas an Yeth Kernewek (Fellowship of the Cornish Language). An annual Pan-Celtic Festival at Killarney encourages the writing and performing of songs in the language; Cornish language magazines are published, Yeth an Weryn (Language of the People) evenings are held, at which conversation and song can be practised; church services are widely held in the language, with the encouragement of Nonconformist churches and the Diocese of Truro; plays have been revived and performed in it, and to an ever-growing body of modern literature there was added, in 1984, the first novel in the Cornish language, by Bard Abransek (W. Melville Bennetto): *An Gurun Wosek a Geltya* – The Bloody Crown of Keltia.

Although the tongue is still spoken and written by only a small (though ever-growing) minority, about a thousand people at the present time, few regard it as a joke. It is used officially on occasions, and the annual brochure of the Cornish Tourist Board gives it deferential treatment. Most would agree that the revival has brought credit to Cornwall and that it would have been a tragedy to lose this attractive and poetic Celtic tongue.

Little has survived in Cornwall of the second great Celtic Festival of the year, Samhain (made Christian under the name of All Hallows or All Saint's Day) except the ill-defined idea of lanterns and ghosts at Hallowe'en. At Samhain (pronounced Sawain) the Celtic year ended and began, the dead and living intermingled, and the gods walked abroad. The traditional Samhain bonfires have become merged with Guy Fawkes Night celebrations on 5 November, but apart from the fireworks there seems no good reason to celebrate the explosive Mr Fawkes in this way. A race-memory survives here, harking back to Celtic times and before.

At the Feast of St Just in Penwith, held on the Sunday nearest to Hallowe'en, the 'Allan Apple', taken to bed by children the previous night, is eaten on awakening; something which seems to symbolize the fruit harvest. The Feast itself used to be a great extravagance: beef, fowls in butter and parsley, streaky pork, vegetables, rabbit pie and figgy (plum) pudding, with brandy and toddy to follow for the men, and 'sweet-drink' – mead – for the women and children. There appears here a shadow of the Samhain feasts at which cattle were killed off, except for a few kept for breeding.

And so to winter and Christmas. Cornish cottagers down the centuries have been amused and instructed by wandering droll-tellers, many of whose age-old tales were collected by William Bottrell, Robert Hunt and others. Such stories and legends were treasured by the older folk, but after the Education Act of 1872 the children seem to have lost their taste for such innocent myths.

Yet folklore dies hard. Succeeding generations have been well served by antiquarians like M. A. Courtnay, T. Q. Couch, Thurston Peter and Robert Morton Nance, who recorded and published dialect sayings, legends of saints, piskies, mermaids, giants, cures and superstitions. Today these continue in local publications and the occasional play enacted by travelling groups of actors, and still fascinate an amused, if less credulous, public.

Mummers' plays were popular in Cornwall down to about 1890. Rough and ready, with bucolic humour and songs, they were part of Christmas festivities, when troupes would go from farm to farm, village to village, presenting St George and the Turkish Knight, or St George and the Dragon, collecting their Christmas boxes and being given refreshment. Some scattered revivals at folk clubs and Cornish events have since taken place. Guise dancing was a great feature in west Cornwall; in 1831 at Penzance it was likened to an Italian carnival, with girls dressed as boys and vice versa, all with blackened faces or masks; everyone in the town, high and low, took part. St Ives and the Isles of Scilly were also noted for these 'humorous and piquant' events at Christmas and the New Year.

But the greatest contribution the Cornish have made to the celebration of Christmas is surely the unique and inimitable tradition of Cornish carols, or 'curls' as they are known in west Cornwall. These four-part songs date from the early Methodist and Evangelistic revivals; there is a theory that they are actually adaptations or developments of the 'three men's songs' mentioned by Carew. Be that as it may, the power and exquisite melodies of these carols never fail to impress. Some of them are the work of known composers such as Thomas Merritt of Illogan (the best loved of them, whose genius was recognized in the 1970s by Dr Malcolm Arnold), Stephen Nicholas and Thomas Broad of Redruth; others have grown like folksongs, to a kind of perfection unknown within the strict rules of musical composition, and are sung with religious fervour at Padstow, at Morwenstow and in west Cornwall. In our own day the carols of Kenneth Pelmear are gaining many adherents. Best heard in the open air, with crowds of carollers releasing their joy to the angelic skies, singing less to regale an audience than to express their own seasonal delight, they bring us back to a world of primitive worship and Nonconformist emotion – the Celtic passion which two centuries ago became converted to the Way of the Wesleys, Whitefield and the Cornish Bible Christian leader O'Bryan.

7 The Cornishman's Religion

Of the ancient religions of Cornwall, from the Mesolithic to the Bronze Age, we know little, and we can only make speculations according to what facts we have (some of these have been set out in Chapter 1). The pre-Christian Celts left more indications, however, and in the St Columb Hurling (Imbolc), the Padstow and Helston May celebrations and the midsummer bonfires (Beltaine), we have relics of two of their great festivals. The third, Lugnasad, may be represented by 'Crying the Neck', and Samhain survives, much altered, in Hallowe'en and Guy Fawkes customs. What gods the Celts worshipped are known to us from a variety of sources, and it is safe to assume that some at least had their devotees in Cornwall and Dumnonia: Lugh, the Lord of Skills and Unleasher of Lightning, Cernunnos, god of fertility and the underworld, Epona, the horse goddess, the fruitful Matres (a trio of goddesses), Tarannis, god of thunder, and Dagda, the 'Good God', a father-figure of immense virility, and many others.

The Celts also had a host of local deities, the spirits of pools, springs and wells, groves and cairns; some of these sites, especially the wells, were later adapted to Christian use. The strong belief of Britons in the afterlife – recorded as even promising to repay debts after death – was a recurrent theme in all their religious dealings; their lives were governed by invocations to, and fears of, various supernatural forces and beings, and also by what would now be called superstitions but which were part of a strictly observed way of living with powers over which they had no control. These 'superstitions' still exert influence over country people today. The white witch or charmer still operates, curing skin diseases by 'charming' garments worn by the sufferer; many a case of their success, incredible though they may seem to modern ears, can be told in the villages and hamlets up and down Cornwall. *Geists* or taboos, laid on heroes and even tribes, have their echoes in superstitions such as that of not bringing flowering hawthorn (may) into one's house, bearing an ash branch to keep snakes away, throwing salt over one's left shoulder and never saying 'rabbit' when in a boat.

Cross at Lanteglos (Camelford)

The ascendancy of Rome caused Britons to venerate Roman gods also, in some cases identifying their own traditional deities with Jove, Mars, Venus etc. But when, in the fifth century AD, the Romans left, there was a return to the purer tribal religions. It may, however, be of the greatest significance that Arthur, when rallying the Britons against the advance of Germanic peoples some sixty or seventy years later, is reputed to have carried into battle a shield on which was depicted the Virgin holding her Child. Whether this was a pious piece of publicity, or whether Arthur himself was a devout Christian, we may never know. But there had been Christians in Britain at least since the third century AD, and they had gained a fair following in the western provinces and in Wales; now, with the collapse of the Roman Empire, which must have seemed like the approaching end of their world, many Britons turned to this new religion. With the peace won by Arthur and his twelve victories, which lasted some forty or more years in the sixth century, much progress was made in the south-west peninsula by Irish and Welsh missionaries, many of whom also went on to proselytize Brittany, where so many south-western Celts had settled. Later numbers of Armorican or Breton holy men came over to Cornwall to spread the Gospel, especially around the Fal estuary, and some local Cornish saints also established their cells.

After the conversion of Ireland by St Patrick in the early fifth century, a wave of Irish missionaries came to west Cornwall, including St Breaca (Breage), St Ia (St Ives), and St Fingar (Gwinear). Many of them are said to have been killed by Tewdr (Theodore), Prince of Meneage. Meanwhile in Wales important monasteries had been founded and now sent out another generation of abbots and bishops, like St Carantoc (Crantock), St Cadoc (Quethiock), St Samson (Golant and South Hill, and Dol in Brittany), St Brioc (St

Celtic Cross, Lelant churchyard

Breock and St Brieuc) and scores, if not hundreds, of others. St David is commemorated at Davidstow, and his mother, St Nonna, at Altarnun and Pelynt.

But the greatest of the Welsh missionaries was St Petroc. He founded monasteries at Padstow and Bodmin and travelled over a wide area of Cornwall, Devon, Somerset and Brittany, founding churches. (There are, in fact, twenty-four dedications to him in Devon.) His influence was enormous, and it is not surprising that his name and foundations have survived down to the present day, whilst numerous obscure Celtic saints with small cells have in the course of time been forgotten and their churches re-dedicated to other, more fashionable saints. That the conversion of the Cornish and south-western Celts was genuine is supported by the fact that so much land was given to the new monasteries by landowners, chiefs and local kings; St Petroc received lands from Constantine, a north Cornish prince whom he converted, and, according to Leland, also King Tewdr, who perhaps repented of his massacre of Irish saints.

From this time dates the erection or re-dedication of the Cornish granite crosses, which are found in profusion west of the Tamar (there are only a few in Devon). St Samson is credited with carving a cross on a phallic stone, the centre of celebrations – perhaps at Lugnasad, when horse races were held – during which a youth was killed. Having demonstrated the superior power of Christianity by reviving the boy, St Samson converted the very symbol of their local rites. Thus began the long tradition which continues today in the form of war memorials and headstones. In the seventh and eighth centuries were set up impressive wheel-headed crosses like Long Tom at Minions, St Piran's Cross at Perranzabuloe, and the Mylor churchyard cross, tallest in Cornwall.

A later type, found mainly in west Cornwall, has a rudely sculptured Christ figure with outstretched arms on one face; there are excellent examples at Sancreed and St Buryan. Most of these crosses denote a preaching place, for only later did the idea of a permanent church building take hold. Some seem to have been raised as guideposts for travellers, like Carminnow Cross and one at Washaway, both near Bodmin. Some of the later crosses bear inscriptions; near Tintagel is an eighth-century one with the Saxon legend 'Aelnat made this cross for his soul.' Such crosses were still being erected in the fifteenth century.

Like Ireland, Wales and Brittany, Cornwall is rich in holy wells dedicated to the saints of their localities; there are nearly two hundred of them, and they bear witness to the importance that life-giving water, the medium of baptism, held for these Celtic Christians. Some were restored in later times with now-venerable well-housings, as at St Keyne, St Clether, Dupath and St Cleer. Others like Madron have been left in their pristine state, still, however, today an object of veneration and superstition.

Many Cornish churches were built inside former Iron Age rounds. The prefix *lan* (sacred enclosure) denotes an ancient Celtic foundation; according to Charles Henderson, 98 of 254 Cornish parishes must have had a large or small group of cells composed of huts, within such establishments. We can glimpse the form they took from various excavations, especially on Tintagel island (the earliest of them, perhaps late fifth century). There would be the cell of the abbot or bishop, cells for individual monks, and perhaps for the prior or priest-in-charge, a *hospitum* for travellers, a refectory, a school, a storehouse or granary and later a *scriptorium* where holy texts were copied out.

This loosely knit system of *lans* (small monasteries), interlinked but not dominated by any one abbot or bishop, suited the Celts, who, as we have seen, lived in *trefs* and hamlets and had no true towns. It was a life of strict and often harsh asceticism, devoted to prayer, tilling the soil, fishing, animal husbandry and good works. The Latin lives of SS Petroc, Samson, Crantock, Piran and others, although dating from later ages, give a picture which cannot be doubted of devoted brotherhoods led in each case by a beloved holy father, whose name was to be venerated down the centuries.

As the Dark Ages fell on Europe and the rest of Britain, these and their successors worked on, spreading the Gospel, holding together in peace communities of devout people, for the Celts were always religious, living half in the Other World; and Christianity was to them a refining and fulfilment of the creed instilled into them a thousand years of Druidism – which, apart from its sacrificial rites, had had so much to commend itself.

Although after St Augustine landed in Kent in 597 the Roman Church gradually extended itself in the wake of the Germanic conquests, the Celtic Church in Cornwall did not submit for some centuries to the rule of the Papacy. It was not until Egbert's victory over the Cornish and Danes at Hingston Down in 838 that the Catholic persuasion began to gain ground west of the Tamar. In 850 the last Celtic abbot-bishop, Kenstec, who seems to have had his seat at Bodmin, acknowledged the rule of Canterbury. The Bodmin and Padstow monasteries were left undisturbed, though Egbert created some important estates out of monastic lands, including the great manor of Pawton (possibly 'Petrockton') which spread over several parishes to the west of the Camel estuary.

In 931 Athelstan created the diocese of Cornwall, fixing its seat at St Germans, diplomatically naming a Cornishman, Conan, its first

Altarnun Church and Bridge

bishop. During the years 940 to 1040 manumissions (records of liberation) of slaves were recorded in the illuminated Gospels in Bodmin Church: the shrine of St Petroc being held by Saxons and Celts alike to be the most venerable of places for such purposes. Of 122 names 98 are Celtic and only twelve are Saxon or English. Evidently the latter had seized large estates in east and mid Cornwall and were now being prevailed upon to free slaves taken on their arrival. All the main offices and treasures of the Padstow monastery were moved inland to Bodmin after Padstow was sacked by the Vikings in 981.

New foundations were endowed by the English and Norman kings: a Benedictine house at Tywardreath (before 1154) and one at Minster near Boscastle, about 1165; St Michael's Mount, previously a Celtic monastery, was reconstituted and given to Mont Saint-

Mylor Church

Michel on the Brittany coast. Meanwhile the See of St Germans was merged with the Devon bishopric of Crediton, and in 1050 this itself was moved to Exeter, which was then to rule large areas of Cornwall, its Church lands and monastic foundations, until the diocese of Truro was established in 1876. A college of canons was established at St Germans, and the manor and lands passed into the hands of the Norman bishops. Other colleges were established at St Buryan, Crantock and St Endellion. In the thirteenth century the Augustinians established themselves in Cornwall with a monastery at Launceston, and the same order took over Bodmin Priory; they built a new church wherein the relics of St Petroc were housed. In 1259 Bishop Bronscombe consecrated the Dominican friary at Truro, and in 1264 he founded Glasney College at Penryn, which was to be a centre of learning and teaching, a sort of proto-university.

The old Celtic monasticism had ended, though most of the parishes created by the bishops were centred on their foundations.

Norman priests were now in charge of new solid stone churches. The power of the Exeter bishops was immense. The office was usually granted to a relative or favourite of the ruling monarch, and some of them visited Cornwall only rarely, being much concerned with affairs of state; for instance, Walter Stapledon was Edward II's Treasurer, and Bishop Stafford was Chancellor to Richard II. Some 135 Norman churches soon replaced the Saxon or Celtic structures, and we can see some of their work today at Tintagel, with its thick walls and narrow windows, Morwenstow, with its strong round pillars, St Germans, with its two magnificent towers, and St Anthony in Roseland, still in its original cruciform shape with tower over the crossing.

The cult of relics became a great feature of medieval religion in Cornwall, as elsewhere. At St Germans the relics of St Germanus of Auxerre were acquired by dubious means; at Bodmin were those of St Petroc, so richly rewarding to the town; at Perranzabuloe the head and leg bones of St Piran, and at St Michael's Mount the milk of the Virgin Mary, no less. Sir Roger Wallysborough, shipwrecked near the Lizard whilst returning from a pilgrimage to the Holy Land, commemorated his survival by presenting Grade Church with a piece of the Holy Cross which he was bringing back with him. It was an age of widespread credulity, with the Church all powerful and all-pervading. St Piran's relics, carried 'up and down the country' (Nicholas Roscarrock), annoyed other parishes, draining off their alms. The famous fracas in Bodmin Church in 1113, between locals and canons from Laon in France, occurred when the canons arrived on a begging tour with relics of Our Lady; a blind girl touched them and was said to be cured. (The row itself was over whether King Arthur would return.) Then in 1177 the relics of St Petroc were stolen and taken to Saint-Méen, after a great outcry they were returned by Henry II, overlord of Brittany, in the priceless ivory reliquary still to be seen in Bodmin Church.

The middle and late fourteenth century was a time of great unrest. The Church was growing rich at the expense of the laity, and open to many corruptions. Tithes appropriated by the bishops impoverished whole parishes. The Black Death spread after 1384, taking some twenty thousand lives in Cornwall of a population of seventy thousand or so, including many priests, and the priors of Bodmin, Minster and St Michael's Mount. Goods became scarce and prices rose. The resulting civil discontent produced violence towards priests: one was killed at Poundstock in 1357, another at St Hilary in 1380. The preaching of heretics spread further discontent; weakened by rival Popes, the Papacy lost much authority. Few people could follow the Latin services, and often business was transacted during

Roche Rock

Mass. Many priests were openly living with women as their 'housekeepers'.

Various foundations got into trouble at this period. Bodmin Priory was in debt. At Launceston the prior was suspended and then deprived; Bishop Stafford's register of the late years of the century recorded severe penances laid upon canons there for immorality. At Crantock part of the college was turned into a tavern. Priests deeply resented the friars, whom they considered usurped their functions and alms. Pluralism was widespread; although it was condemned by Rome, the Exeter bishops often allowed the holding of more than one living. Often the rector would be non-resident, taking service with some rich family or studying at Oxford, paying a poor vicar a miserable pittance to run his parish.

There was an economic revival and a more zealous attitude to religion in the fifteenth century. The expansion of the wool trade and of mining brought money to rebuild most of the Cornish churches between 1410 and 1530; the old Norman churches were largely replaced by those in Gothic styles, most being enlarged by the addition of aisles and chapels. Towers were rebuilt at the western end instead of being over the crossing. New pillars and arcades in Cataclews, Polyphant and Pentewan stone, and magnificent stained and painted glass windows (of which today only St Neot's survive); wall paintings in blazing colours, some of which can be seen restored at Breage, Poughill, Linkinhorne and Morwenstow; and a profusion of intricately carved bench ends by local craftsmen, as at Altarnun, Davidstow, Cardinham, St Winnow, Mullion and other churches – all bear witness to the resurgence of civic pride and spiritual devotion, for the medieval church was the community centre of its day. Bodmin Church was rebuilt during 1469–91; Probus and St Austell, with ornately worked granite towers, followed, and St Mary Magdalene, Launceston, benefited from the widowed Sir Henry Trecarrel, who abandoned his new manor house in order to finance it.

There was also a return to the eremitic life. Chapels and cells for hermits were licensed at Roche Rock, Roughtor, Padstow (St Saviour's Point), near Restormel Castle, Bede Haven (Bude) and Marhamchurch, where the anchoress Cecilia Moyes lived in a cell attached to the church. The gentry built chapels at their own manor houses and often had their own priests. The spiritual life, it seemed, under the Roman Catholic Church, was now supreme.

Yet within a few years it was under severe attack from the Crown of England. Henry VIII followed Luther and Calvin in renouncing the Pope's authority and established the Church of England with himself as its Head, thus enabling himself to marry whom he pleased.

The King soon cast his eyes on the rich monastic properties and in 1536 seized the minor foundations, the friaries in 1538 and the large monasteries in 1539. The chantries fell a few years later, in the reign of Edward VI. The deprived monks were offered livings under the new Church, or a pension of £6 per annum. The priors did much better, getting from £60 to £100 a year. The monastic buildings were sold or leased out to fill the state coffers, and soon decayed, their stone being used for much other building, so that little remains today of the important houses at Glasney, Bodmin, Truro and Launceston. There were to be no more pilgrimages, no displays of relics; images in churches were defaced and wall paintings and furnishings destroyed.

At the time of Henry's death in 1547 a new order of service and prayer book, both in English, were being devised. These were to become law by the Act of Uniformity of 1549, against which the Catholics of Cornwall came out in open revolt.

The Prayer Book Rebellion actually began in Devon, but the staunchly Catholic Cornish gentry soon joined it with their priests and servants and crossed the Tamar to besiege Exeter. The government of the boy King Edward was shaken by the revolt, which was put down only with the aid of German mercenaries, who won a

Octagonal spire of St Bartholomew's Church, Lostwithiel

narrow victory. But this victory, followed by ruthless justice administered by the Provost Marshall, Sir Anthony Kingston, suppressed Catholic aspirations; the leaders, including the vicars of St Veep and Poundstock, were executed, and the rebel gentry lost their estates.

However, the Catholics had a last respite when Edward died and his sister Mary succeeded him. Mary tried to put the clock back, threw out the English Prayer Book, brought in the old usages and the Latin Mass and replaced those Protestant bishops opposing her with loyal Catholics. Clergy who had married were either deprived or given another living if they renounced their wives. It might have worked if Mary had not persecuted those who wanted to remain Protestant. Many were hounded into exile; Agnes Prest of Boyton on the Tamar was burned as a heretic at Exeter. The whole country was torn by religious strife, which Mary's marriage to Philip of Spain exacerbated, raising the spectre of Spanish domination.

But Mary died in 1558 and Elizabeth came to the throne; the life of Catholics became, over the next several decades, more and more difficult. The Roscarrocks, Tregians, Arundells of Lanherne and others might have been left in comparative peace had not the 'Roaring Bull' from Rome in 1570 declared Elizabeth excommunicated and deposed; henceforth they were considered potential traitors. Soon, refusing to attend the parish church and take part in the new services, they paid dearly in fines and sequestrations of their property. Recusant priests visited them, clandestinely administering the Mass; in 1577 Cuthbert Mayne was discovered at Golden and,

St Just in Roseland

after a show trial hanged, drawn and quartered at Launceston. (Mayne was canonized in 1972.) Francis Tregian went to the tower and died in exile; Nicholas Roscarrock was thrown into various London prisons, where he wrote his *Lives of the British Saints*.

Despite the odds against them, some Cornish Catholics clung on to their faith; in 1671 there were sixty-seven of them, mainly on the old Arundell estates. They continued steadfast until a more tolerant age dawned at the end of the eighteenth century. One of them, Richard Rawe of Rialton in St Columb Minor, treasured the head of Cuthbert Mayne, which he was later able to present to a Carmelite convent at Lanherne in 1794.

Meanwhile, though the Anglican Church established itself in the place of the Roman Catholic Church, only eighty years or so after Elizabeth's accession another state of affairs ensued: the Church of England was now considered by the Puritan Parliamentarians to be too lax and catholic. Dissenting sects grew; by the time of the Civil War there were in Cornwall Presbyterians, Independents, Congregationalists, Baptists, Anabaptists and others. Under the Commonwealth the Anglican clergy were replaced by these Puritans of various hues. Cornwall, with much of the rest of the country, passed through another period of upheaval and stress. Still suspecting new ways, the Cornish laity found their churches desecrated, the stained glass windows smashed, crosses and rood screens destroyed, and organs dismantled; even civil marriages and lay registers of births and deaths were introduced. An entry in the register of Launceston church reads, '27th November 1655. Hereafter follow marriages by laymen, according to the profaneness and giddyness of the times, without precedent or example in any Christian Kingdom or Commonwealth from the Birth of Christ to this very year.'

After Cromwell's death in 1658 it was Sir John Grenville of Stow who prevailed upon his cousin General Monk to invite the exiled Charles II to return. Under the Restoration of the monarchy the Anglican clergy, who had suffered great deprivations, returned to their cures, and fifty Puritan ministers chose a life of itinerant preaching and organizing their dissenting followers rather than accept the new prayer book and liturgy of 1662. Nonconformity was in fact illegal until 1689, and though they had to attend church service, many protested: Quakers would wear their hats in church and refuse to sing or pray aloud. Thomas Tregoss, ejected from Mylor and Mabe, was imprisoned and fined for holding meetings, but the Independent William Oliver at Launceston was able to preach undisturbed and by 1718 had 130 regular attendants at his gatherings. At Helston, Jago, the former Puritan vicar of Wendron, was even able to preach in the church. There were six dissenting ministers at Saltash.

George Fox, founder of the Society of Friends, was imprisoned in Launceston Gaol in 1655, for publishing a manifesto. This led to considerable interest in the Quaker faith, and the Society began to spread in Cornwall. Despite various persecutions by the law (for instance, Ann Upcott of St Austell was on her brother's evidence beaten and put in the stocks for mending a garment on a Sunday), by 1700 there were twenty-seven meeting-houses and four hundred members; Loveday Hambly of Tregongreeves near St Austell and Thomas Mounce of Liskeard were prominent supporters; both of them had suffered imprisonment. Although the Friends never attained a large following, the Quaker Fox family of St Budock had a considerable impact on Cornish life: not only did they prosper in business and mining ventures but they were exemplary employers, and two of their women, Caroline and Anna Maria, founded the Royal Cornwall Polytechnic Society at Falmouth, which did much good work in the mid and later nineteenth century, including studies

St Merryn Church

of the wretched working conditions in order to urge improvements. Baptists also had a strong following during the eighteenth and nineteenth centuries, holding their immersions in the sea at Padstow, Helston and Falmouth.

After the Restoration, the Church of England became well entrenched, its incumbents now being members of the gentry and often possessing land of their own. Pluralism and absenteeism were still common; in 1779 there were fifty-seven non-resident clergymen holding livings in Cornwall, against eighty-nine who were resident. Some, like Dr William Borlase, held two parishes (the worthy doctor claimed he needed both to maintain his family). The Age of Reason had arrived, and the general attitude among the middle and upper classes was that all things had now been ordered for the best.

But the Church signally failed to maintain contact with the many thousands of workers in the new cities and expanding towns, and the emergence of Methodism and Evangelism was directly concerned with ministering to these artisans and their families. John Wesley and his followers found fruitful ground in Cornwall, where the mining populations of St Austell, Redruth, Camborne and St Just

'Come to Good' Quaker meeting house, Feock

and the fisherfolk of St Ives, Mevagissey, Padstow, etc., were ill served by the Church. It was to these emotional and naïve Cornish people that they preached. Charles Wesley in his journal of July 1743 wrote at St Ives: 'I spoke to some of these loving simple people, who are as sheep in the midst of wolves. The Priests stir up the people, and make their minds evil affected towards the brethren.'

The Wesleys and George Whitefield had no revolutionary doctrine, being ordained ministers of the Anglican Church, but from the first they encountered suspicion and hostility from the clergy and squires. Mobs were stirred up against them; they faced accusations of supporting the Jacobites, and violent scenes including stone-throwing confronted them at St Ives, Gwennap, Port Isaac and elsewhere. 'Mad' Squire Eusticke of Botallack is said to have driven his pack of hounds in among Charles Wesley's congregation.

But the tinners and fishermen had found their true voice. Here, instead of aloof prelates preaching obscure theology, were men of fire and passion assuring their hearers that every one of them was important in the sight of God and that through devotion to Jesus Christ they would obtain everlasting life in heavenly bliss, whatever their wretched state in this world. After the failure of the '45 Rebellion there was less opposition, and various sympathetic vicars invited the Methodists to preach from their pulpits. Open-air meetings, hitherto proscribed, grew rapidly; Gwennap Pit was adapted by miners for John Wesley to preach in, which he did on his visits from 1763 to 1790. He came thirty-two times to Cornwall, travelling on horseback in all weathers; chambers for him and his fellow preaches were built at Trewint near Altarnun, Crantock and Trewellard near St Just. Charles' great hymns were eagerly embraced by the fervently singing Celts of Cornwall; 'Come, Divine Immanuel, Come' was written at Land's End.

John Wesley himself never left the Church of England. He resisted increasing pressures to secede, though late in his career he did allow certain Methodist preachers to administer the Sacrament. But after his death in 1791 the Wesleyans broke away from the Anglicans, and soon a growing number of other sects were established. In 1815 William Bryan of Luxulyan (he later spelt his name O'Bryan) formed his own connexion, known as the Bible Christians. These 'Bryanites' soon obtained a large following and built scores of their own chapels up and down the Duchy. After O'Bryan had gone to America to continue his work there, preachers like Billy Bray of Twelveheads carried on this most emotional and revivalistic type of religion, so scorned by Robert Hawker and other established clergy. The preachers' doctrine of 'Free Grace', it seemed to them, was especially dangerous, an excuse to backslide into depravity with the knowledge that by becoming 'converted' again at the next meeting all would be forgiven.

But the tremendous work done by Billy Bray and others recalls the effects of Wesley himself on these naïve but true-hearted people. Bible Christianity was a direct, readily accepted appeal to the heart and soul, and the downtrodden and ignored Cornish were ready for it. It burned deep into the memories and affections of the people and is not forgotten today. By the end of the nineteenth century the various factions were coming together, and in 1932 the three main denominations – the Wesleyans, Primitives and Bible Christian Methodists – were united into a single Methodist Church.

The effect of Wesley and his successors on Cornish (and indeed British) life was vast. In one way, however, it perpetuated the social system, preventing revolution as in France by directing the attention

Centenary Wesleyan Church, Camborne

of the working class to the next world rather than this. But the Nonconformist concern which resulted from it led to pressure for reforms and forced the Church of England to re-examine its role; conscientious vicars and curates did much good work among the poor, and improvements in mining and factory conditions, and the spread of education, can be directly or indirectly related to the new religious movements.

It is sometimes claimed that Methodism inhibited smuggling and wrecking, both of which Wesley deplored. But often smugglers like John Carter, 'the King of Prussia Cove', were actually Wesleyans, and the decline of smuggling was rather due to the stricter enforcement of the law after the Napoleonic Wars. Wrecking – the despoiling of foundered ships – continued until enough Excise officers could prevent it; but the aroused conscience of coastal dwellers, both Anglican and Methodist, brought about great efforts to save vessels in danger, and lifeboats were put into service through voluntary local subscription, one of the earliest being at Padstow in 1822. Wesley himself never forbade the drinking of alcohol, but the great Temperance movement which came into being in the 1830s was from the first associated with Nonconformity.

Faced with the overwhelming successes of Methodism and Nonconformity, many in the Church of England turned to the High Church ritualist party – Robert Hawker (who wore an alb and chasuble at the Eucharist) being one of the foremost. Others supported the Evangelical or Low Church movement. As a new bishop at Exeter in 1831, Henry Phillpotts made a great impact; the number of resident clergy soon rose markedly, and with the spread of Church Sunday Schools there was a large increase in confirmations. Music now became much more important in churches; choirs were formed, to be led by large pipe organs instead of the old instrumental groups; they sang *Hymns Ancient and Modern* and even some of Charles Wesley's in certain parishes. New churches for growing communities at Baldhu, Pendeen, St Day and some twenty-seven other parishes were built during Phillpott's episcopacy.

Most of the older churches were restored at this time, after a period of great neglect due to the ineffectiveness of the Church Rate. 'Restoration' often involved a ruthless scraping away and sometimes wanton destruction of bench ends and screens, as in the work of J. P. St Aubyn, though a number of architects, among them G. E. Street and J. Sedding, dealt sensitively with late medieval buildings. The Church Rate, levied on Anglican and Nonconformist alike, was a great cause of resentment; relations between the Churches improved considerably after its abolition in 1869. The climax of the Anglican revival came, of course, with the building of Truro Cathedral and the

Wesley Memorial Chapel, Gwennap Pit

St Austell Church

re-creation of the Cornish diocese, which was enacted in 1876; the following year Bishop (later Archbishop) Benson was enthroned.

Meanwhile Roman Catholics, emancipated in 1829, had been quietly increasing in number. *Emigrés* from the French Revolution brought priests and nuns with them; Sir Harry Trelawny, Vicar of Egloshayle, 'went over' to Rome in 1834, and Irish immigrants joining the mining and railway booms brought more adherents into Cornwall. Missions at Falmouth, Penzance and Bodmin were suc-

Memorial to Billy Bray, Baldhu churchyard

cessful between 1820 and 1846, when William Young, the 'Apostle of Cornwall' opened a chapel at Bodmin. In 1850 a new Catholic see was established at Plymouth, serving Devon and Cornwall. The controversial death-bed conversion of Robert Stephen Hawker in 1875 added publicity and perhaps converts. New Catholic churches, sometimes of imaginative design, as at St Stephen's by Launceston and the quietly impressive abbey at Bodmin, have enhanced the Roman presence.

Today there is a strong and still growing interest in maintaining the fabric of Cornish churches, of whatever persuasion; though many parishes have been merged together, and hundreds of chapels have been closed. Gwennap Pit still draws hundreds to its services, especially on Spring Bank Holiday. The Society of Friends meet at their simple houses from Penzance to Saltash, and especially at their beautiful thatched cottage at Come-to-Good near Truro. Baptists, Pentecostalists, Congregationalists, Spiritualists, Christian Scientists, Latter Day Saints (Mormons), Seventh Day Adventists and Unitarians meet at various towns. The manifold strands of religion in Cornwall are as multi-coloured as ever, each persuasion bearing in its own way witness to man's continuing need for worship, goodness and peace of soul.

8 The Cornishman's Work

Throughout their history the Cornish have been miners, farmers and fishermen, and today these industries still bring in a great part of Cornwall's earnings. Considered along with the immense mineral wealth of china clay, granite and slate, and the tourist trade based on the soft climate and incomparable scenery, it seems a cruel paradox that wages in Cornwall are so low – about half the UK national average – and that a fifth of its workforce are unemployed in winter. Cornish people have not on the whole complained overmuch, though they have done their share of rioting and rebelling in lean times. In recent centuries their answer to depressions has been emigration, mainly to other mining areas around the globe, where many of them have prospered instead of starving at home. Today that response is increasingly difficult to make, as the new countries which the Cornish helped to build up close their doors to new immigrants.

The romance of tin-mining has fascinated authors since Diodorus Siculus, and to the Cornish themselves tin and copper have always held out the great possibility of sudden riches: the idea of finding a 'keenly lode' (striking a bonanza) still haunts the Cornish consciousness, though in general it was not the working tinner who grew rich but the financiers or 'adventurers'. Tin-working began in the Bronze Age, when it was seen that where streams cut across moors they often exposed veins of the black ore and produced heavy dark pebbles which could be smelted down to produce tin, one of the components of bronze.

The ancient tin-trade is obscured by legends and unanswered questions. Tin was certainly sought from Britain, according to Strabo and other classical writers, who spoke of the Cassiterides, the Tin Isles; the Phoenicians are said to have come to trade here. But it is much more likely that the tin reached Massalia (now Marseilles), which was a Phoenician colony, by the overland route from Brittany. According to Diodorus, Ictis, an island off the British coast, was the chief place where ingots of tin were to be bought. Arguments and theories abound as to whether St Michael's Mount, the Isle of Wight or even the Isle of Thanet was intended.

The Romans, although they established camps in Cornwall, were not overmuch concerned with tin, having ample supplies from Lusitania (Spain); Cornish tin interested them perhaps as an alternative source. Tin-streaming continued during the Dark Ages, but in such unsettled times there was small demand for it. By the end of the twelfth century, however, the kings of England were looking to both Cornish and Devon tin as a likely source of revenue. William de Wrotham, appointed in 1197 as Warden of the Stannaries, came down and drew up a series of laws to regulate the tin trade. In this he had the good sense to consult the working tinners of the time; the code was confirmed by King John in the first Stannary Charter of 1201, which recognized certain prescriptive rights (i.e. rights enjoyed by them before records began). One of the most important was that of bounding – staking one's claim to dig for tin, or to work tin streams; others were the right to work without let or hindrance on the lands of 'bishops, abbots and counts' – which meant practically anywhere in Cornwall; and to divert streams for their works. In other words, tinners were to be given a very free hand, so that the state would benefit from their production. A second charter, of 1305 (Edward I), granted, or confirmed, further privileges, including exemption of miners from all taxes and tolls, except the duty on refined tin itself.

The metal was increasingly used during the fourteenth and fifteenth centuries for military cannon, church plate, brass memorials and pewter utensils, and output grew accordingly. Although the Cornish revolted in 1497 against Henry VII's taxes to finance his Scottish war, and lost their tin charters, they were allowed to buy them back in 1508, when they were granted the Great Charter. This confirmed previous privileges and in addition gave them the right to hold their own Parliament. The Stannaries were vested in the Duchy of Cornwall.

The Cornish Convocation (Stannary Parliament) extended the class of privileged tinner, exempt from all Crown taxes, to all who worked at smelting, carrying and trading in tin. The Stannary Charters have never been revoked; they are *de jure*, if not *de facto*, law even today. But the Crown imposed a duty of 4 shillings per hundredweight, payable on coining the bars of smelted tin (French *coin*, a corner, which was chiselled off to be assayed and approved); and the establishment of pre-emption (the right of the Crown to have first choice of tin to buy, at 'a reasonable and fixed rate' – in effect creating a price ring) did not improve the lot of the working tinner. Except in the days of the Commonwealth, when coinage was abolished, they often lived from hand to mouth, having to borrow until

Bosigran Engine House

quarter day when their tin would be assayed and bought. Coinage was finally abolished in 1838.

Meanwhile, streamed tin no longer meeting the demand, mechanical mining improvements had become necessary in order to go deeper underground. Techniques were still primitive; in Carew's day they used picks, hammers and iron wedges, sometimes heating the rock surface by fire to split it open. (Gunpowder was introduced, with several tragic results, in 1689.) Some mines reached a depth of fifty fathoms (three hundred feet or nearly a hundred metres), and German engineers were employed to drain the workings: adits (level shafts) were driven into hillsides, and windlasses and waterwheels were used to power pumps. The seventeenth-century bucket pump helped matters, but later the infamous 'rag and chain' pump, worked by relays of men working six-hour spells, took a heavy toll of labourers' lives and health.

Steam power was what eventually made deep mining possible. In 1699 Savery patented a steam pump, and Newcomen's atmospheric engine of 1740 was first used in Wendron parish. By 1778 there were sixty of these slow-stroking machines draining various workings; they used a great quantity of Welsh coal, which was brought to the mines from the coast by trains of packhorses or mules. In 1777 James Watt patented his separate condenser, which was to prove enormously successful in saving coal: five mines around Carharrack in 1779, which had before been using between them seven ponderous Newcomen engines, were re-equipped with five Boulton and Watt machines, effecting a saving of over £10,000 in a single year. Power being greater, shafts were now sunk lower than ever before; copper rather than tin was now the object, being in demand for everything from kettles and kitchenware to copper-bottomed sailing ships. The days of the Copper Kingdom were at hand.

The mine owners, however, now found themselves having to pay Watt a royalty, equivalent of a third of the saving his engines brought them, which they soon resented and began to evade or neglect to pay. From this imposition, as they saw it, they were freed when Watt's monopolistic patent rights expired in 1800. At the same time a revolutionary concept was developed by the Cornish inventors Richard Trevithick and Arthur Woolf: the high-pressure steam-engine, which was varied and improved on by a new generation of mining engineers including the Hornblowers (who came down from Staffordshire), William West and Samuel Grose. It was Woolf who first broke the Boulton and Watt monopoly by constructing an engine with two cylinders – something which Watt had declared would never work. The steam whim, first introduced by Trevithick at Cook's Kitchen in 1805, drastically improved the means of raising the ore to the surface. Stamps – the machinery by which the ore was broken up for smelting – were also soon harnessed to high-pressure steam. By the 1830s mines were being driven deeper than ever before; Dolcoath, at Camborne, had reached around 420 fathoms (it got down to 500 fathoms by the end of the century) – and considerable fortunes were being made by the adventurers. But the lot of the working miner deteriorated rather than improved, since the farther down he had to work, the more hazards he encountered.

The novelist R. M. Ballantyne spent six months in Penwith in 1860, and from his experiences wrote *Deep Down: a Tale of the Cornish Mines*, a startlingly real social document. Ballantyne obviously admired the stoic courage and persistence of the Cornish miners, who in the main got so little for their toil. 'Few of them retain health or strength sufficient to go underground beyond the age of 45, while hundreds of them find an early grave, owing to disease resulting from their peculiar work, or to accidents. These last are usually occasioned by the bursting out of collections of water which

Wheal Coates Engine House, St Agnes

flood the mines; or the fall of masses of timber; or the premature explosion of blast holes. At other times the men lose hold of the ladders – "fall away" from them, as they express it – or stumble into a winze, which is a small shaft connecting level with level, in which case death is almost certain to ensue, many of the winzes being 60 feet deep. In St Just you will see many poor fellows who have been blinded and maimed in the mines.'

Yet, seven years before the book was written, a man-engine was installed at Tresavean; it had been designed by Michael Loam, who had won a prize offered by the Royal Cornwall Polytechnic Society for a device to lift and lower men in the mines. Slowly other mines adopted it, though for far too long so many had to climb up and down ladders, sometimes to three hundred fathoms or more, at each 'core' or shift. Minehead baths and changing-rooms were built; Bickford's safety fuses saved hundreds of lives. But the introduction of the power drill, filling the air with minute particles of dust, resulted in a rapid increase in lung diseases; tuberculosis and phthisis became main hazards. A government commission in 1900 plainly fixed the cause of these, but it was several years before jets and sprays were generally used to keep down the dust. Since the miners' earnings seldom exceeded fifteen shillings a week until the First World War, and they were subject to the varying fortunes of the lodes they worked, few could put anything by. But poverty, disease and insanitary conditions killed more than the fearsome work in the mines themselves.

Meanwhile Cornwall's share of world production of copper had been declining. West Cornwall, full of working mines that raised their granite stacks across the country, especially in the Carnmenellis area south of Redruth, was the hub of the Industrial Age. From 1801 to 1830 Cornish mines produced on average two-thirds of the total world production of fine copper. But other copper areas were being opened up: Chile from the 1830s, soon producing a fifth of world tonnage; then South Australia, where Cornish miners themselves established 'Australia's Little Cornwall' on the Yorke Peninsula; then, in quick succession, the rich copper strikes of Michigan, Montana and Utah. By 1880 copper produced in Cornwall itself accounted for a mere 36,224 tons out of a world figure of 1,189,400.

The collapse of copper resulted in the closure of many mines and a vast exodus of miners, and later of their families, overseas. But a temporary revival in tin-mining in west Cornwall and Caradon kept a key number of workings alive; Botallack was re-opened, only to close again in 1895. In 1919 the rich Levant mine adjacent to it suffered one of the worst Cornish mining accidents, when the man-engine (which had been working for sixty-two years) collapsed and thirty-

Tin miners at work underground, about 1890

one men were killed. Levant itself finally closed in 1930. The marketing of easily won alluvial tin from Malaya and Nigeria caused another slump, and during the 1920s and 30s there was a slow but apparently irreversible decline in the number of mines operating; soon there were fewer than a thousand men working in Cornish mining, whereas a century before over fifty thousand had been employed.

By 1939 only five mines were producing, though two more concerns were re-opened during the Second World War, at Cligga Head, Perranporth (tin and wolfram) and a wolfram mine at Castle an Dinas near St Columb. But in the 1950s the number actually came down to only two: South Crofty at Camborne, and Geevor in St Just. A new era arrived in the 1960s, however, when the world price of tin went up to £6,000 per ton. A cautious revival began, using the latest mining methods: a massive investment was made in Wheal Jane, Baldhu, by Consolidated Goldfields, where the most modern deep tin mine in the world was established, employing over five hundred. With better means of constructing shafts and with electric cable cars, safety helmets and high-powered lubricated drills, the main hazards of the past have been obviated, and today the miner's life is no more dangerous than, say, the fisherman's.

A tin-smelter works at Wheal Jane, where the ore is separated by the froth floatation process, and smelting is by metallurgical means. Mount Wellington, nearby, was re-opened a few years later but closed again in 1979; however, Rio Tinto Zinc, which has taken over Wheal Jane, has been working some parts of this mine. Wheal Pendarves, south-west of Camborne, is worked by South Crofty Ltd: South Crofty itself, which at present employs about 300, is one of the mainstays of the economy of Camborne-Redruth. Geevor, also working part of the old Levant mine, was until recently operating on the clifftop near Land's End, with some of its levels, like those of Botallack, running well out under the sea. A new venture opened in 1983 is Wheal Concord, near Redruth, and planning permission has been given for another on the cliffs at Perranporth. The total worth of tin, zinc, copper, wolfram and other metals won from Cornish mines has recently been in the region of £35 million per year, with the industry employing sixteen hundred highly paid people.

But all this is dependent on the world price of tin remaining sufficiently high to make the expensive Cornish mining ventures profitable. At the time of writing, a huge and terrible question mark hangs over the industry's future, as the floating of prices threatens to cause them to drop below the £6,000 per ton required for viability. Already Geevor has had to make three hundred men redundant, and other companies, though larger and internationally financed, may follow with temporary or permanent closures.

It will have been noticed in a previous chapter that the part played by Cornish quarries down the centuries in providing both work and stone for building churches, bridges and other edifices, has been considerable. Real quarrying dates from the thirteenth century, perhaps before. A great expansion occurred during the time of rebuilding churches in the fifteenth century; the fine dove-grey picrite Polyphant stone from near Launceston was used for arcades and windows of many churches in north and east Cornwall. Buff-coloured elvan from Pentewan quarries was popular in refurbishing the churches of mid-Cornwall, and around the Camel estuary the smooth blue-grey elvan from Cataclewse (*carrek*, rock; *glaze*, *gluz*, grey) near Trevose became something of a celebrated material; fonts, tomb chests and arcades, the first two carved by the Master of Endellion and his apprentices in the mid-fifteenth century, remain objects of great value and admiration.

Slate was worked at Delabole before 1314, when it was used to repair Winchester Castle. Carew (1602) praised the quarry for the lightness, strength and durability of its product. Other slate quarries in north Cornwall opened and flourished from the seventeenth century onwards, producing flooring flags, sills and storage chests as well as helling (roofing) slates; but today Delabole alone continues, its Old Quarry now almost five hundred feet deep. Despite the high price of its slates, the company continues profitably; much of the stone is now used for fine chippings in bitumen roofs, and in power-powdered forms for a variety of industrial fillers.

The granite quarries of north-west Bodmin Moor still supply their stone for memorials, facings and sills; modern cutting technology includes the thermal lance and electric diamond saws. West Penwith, Castle-an-Dinas and Penlee produce crushed roadstone, as do quarries at Luxulyan and Hingston Down further east. But the famed workings at Carnsew, Mabe and Caradon are now silent.

The china-clay industry, which dominates the area around St Austell with mountainous white sandtips, chutes, settling tanks and drying-plants, resulted from the experiments of William Cookworthy, a Plymouth chemist, who found chinastone at Tregonning Hill near Breage in 1746. Cookworthy successfully ground this decomposed granite to a powder and produced pottery from it. As 'pot growan', chinastone had been known to tin-smelters, who lined their furnaces with it. The Tregonning Hill source was impure, but in 1748 Cookworthy found better material on the Hensbarrow granite boss in St Stephen-in-Brannell. As he recorded, this 'petunse' (a Chinese term for the stone) and 'caulin' (kaolin powder) 'produce a much whiter body, and do not shrink so much by far in the baking, nor take stains from the fire'. He had years of experimenting with glazes to do, but doggedly went on trying to produce good china. By 1765 he had established a factory making chinaware at

China clay workers, about 1920

Plymouth and had opened the first china claypits at Carloggas and Rescrowsa to supply it. Later the factory moved to Bristol.

By the time Cookworthy came to renew his patent in 1775, Wedgwood, Spode, Minton and other Staffordshire potters had become interested in the clay. The first Cornish China Clay Company, a partnership between Josiah Wedgwood and John Carthew, was founded in 1782. Charlestown and Par Harbours later facilitated transport to the Potteries, as also did Mevagissey during the early nineteenth century. The Staffordshire men sold out their interests in the Cornish pits, but local merchants and adventurers took their holdings, and as the century progressed more and more pits were opened; about two hundred were operating in 1860, most of them small by today's standards but employing between them seven thousand men, women and children. As tin and copper production fell off, many miners were glad to turn to this less esteemed calling. Carclaze and other mines began to work clay as well as tin, and other pits were opened on Bodmin Moor. At first clay blocks were dried in the open, a lengthy process, but drying-sheds, later to be steam-heated under the floors, were then constructed. Production doubled during 1850 to 1867, reaching 130,000 tons.

By the late 1880s wet clay in solution was being piped down to the driers at Burngullow, and in 1908 John Lovering opened a pipe system to Charlestown for dockside drying. Already Lovering had introduced electricity, first for flood-lighting his pits to enable working by night, and then for a variety of machinery.

Expansion and modernization continued, despite labour troubles and a general clay strike, ruthlessly crushed, in 1919; after 1918 amalgamations and increased investment brought about new methods of extraction, mainly by means of high-powered hoses, and delivery by railway and motor transport. The giant English China Clays set up its own research unit at Charlestown, and its own generating plant. A far greater expansion still was realized after the Second World War, exports of china clay earning Britain valuable currency from abroad (today nearly ninety per cent of refined clay is exported); innumerable products, including paper, cosmetics, pharmaceuticals, paints, insecticides, rubber, plastics, soap and fertilizers now use this bland and ubiquitous, harmless and apparently essential material. Immense driers with rotary kilns have been constructed at Burngullow and Par, working all the year round the clock, sending their unceasing white plumes of smoke and not a little dust into the atmosphere.

Although fewer than forty pits are working today, some are enormous concerns, about four hundred feet deep, producing half a million tons of clay annually. The industry is still the largest single employer in Cornwall, with a workforce of over six thousand, and its ancillary services (building-blocks, heavy transport, joinery etc) employ thousands more.

2,000 feet below ground: the modern pumping station at South Crofty Mine

From the earliest times down to almost the present day, everyone in Cornwall has been involved in some form of farming, or at least in growing their own food or keeping pastoral animals. Not long ago even townspeople conducted these activities in their backyards, on allotments or on common land. At Padstow, Boscastle, St Ives and Mevagissey down to the late nineteenth century the stench of pigs and goats, and the noise of poultry, vied with the smell of boiling pitch and the hammering of caulkers' mallets. Today's divorce between those who farm and those who do not was unknown. The Cornishman may also have been a tinner or fisherman, often both, but he was always some sort of farmer.

The Iron Age Celts, with their tiny fields won from the moorlands, had their own systems of crop rotation and practised mixed farming;

the monks of the Age of the Saints enlarged the tradition with bigger fields, and granaries, and began the market system of trading animals. Parts of their domains came down to later vicars and rectors as glebeland, to be worked by the incumbents or their servants. But the major part of the land became manors under the Saxons and Normans.

Today the manorial system still survives in part: crop-bearing land is still rented out as individual farms by the lord (the largest landowner in Cornwall being the Duke with eighteen estates). Tenancies are no longer limited to a term of the longest of three nominated lives (the usual Cornish system in the past), and their holders are not required to do duty as reeves, bailiffs or wood-wardens or to serve on the lord's juries, since of course the manorial courts of the Middle Ages have long since been abolished. Many farmers today own their land outright, but in medieval times the manorial system ruled all, except the free pastures on hills and moors, which the villeins and burgesses could use.

Two arrangements existed in Cornish agriculture during the Middle Ages: the Celtic groups of small enclosed fields, and the large open Saxon fields divided into strips. The latter was instituted around new settlements; Kilkhampton and Helston are two examples, the long unenclosed strips being worked by various tenants, each having two or three strips worked in rotation so that one always lay fallow: a somewhat wasteful but workable method. The usual Cornish system, dating from pre-Celtic times, was more economical: it was to enclose small, square fields with slate or granite hedges, or earth banks and ditches, in which were grown oats, rye, pillas or wheat. The fields left fallow provided winter hay for animals, which were pastured on the downs in summer. Much of the Cornish landscape, despite large-scale amalgamations of fields and the breaking-in of moorland, was created in this way; the intricate patchwork terrain of small fields is peculiar to the Duchy.

Pastoral farming increased during the later Middle Ages and Tudor times: the mild and wet climate favoured it, for in Cornwall grass grows even in winter, and often two crops of hay can be obtained in a summer. During the seventeenth century sixty per cent of investment by Cornish farmers was in cattle and sheep; in addition to meat and milk, there was a considerable profit in bones, hides, lard and the dung for fertilizer. Gradually horses took over from oxen for ploughing; more winter fodder was grown, clover seeds being a popular import after 1680. Throughout the seventeenth and most of the eighteenth centuries cattle were driven up to Bodmin Moor in large numbers for summer grazing, creating a kind of ranching industry.

Tilling the soil was a lengthy process. Up to the early nineteenth century the preparation of the ground always began, about May, by 'beating up' the soil. The surface was ripped up with beat-axes or velling shears, and the turves were turned back to dry; they were then raked into heaps and burned with furze or stubble to air the soil and get rid of harmful grubs; after that the ashes were spread over the fields and ploughed in with sea-sand, burnt lime, seaweed or fish manure. Many husbandry clauses of tenancy leases over the period 1600 to 1880 specify the exact amounts of sea-sand or lime etc that the landlord required to be ploughed into the land when preparing it in this way; for instance, John Jagoe of Quethiock in 1766 had to put in 120 horse-seams of good salt sea-sand, or fifty bushes of good, well-burnt lime per acre, for each three successive crops of grain.

The introduction of turnips, as a crop to enrich the soil when corn was not sown, was adopted generally elsewhere; but though turnips added nitrogen to the soil, they took much lime from it, and the Cornish did not readily turn to them. Potatoes as a staple crop became essential to the poor. Corn riots occurred in the late eighteenth and early nineteenth centuries, due to scarcity resulting from bad harvests, and the French Wars prevented trade; in 1794–5 frost destroyed most of the potato crop, following the failure of the wheat harvest. At Camelford in 1812 a parish committee guaranteed farmers a fair return, even though the poor paid a reduced price, the difference being borne by the rate-payers: an early welfare scheme not alas emulated elsewhere. In 1842 hungry tinners from St Austell tried to prevent a shipload of grain leaving Wadebridge. During 1846–7 miners and labourers marched on various towns to prevent corn being sent out of Cornwall and to enforce fair prices.

A means of helping the poor to help themselves was introduced by Sir Francis Basset of Tehidy, who encouraged his mining labourers to build themselves cottages and to take in and improve a few acres of 'waste land' – i.e. downs or moors. By this means much of Reskejeage and Treswithian Downs near Camborne were enclosed. Previously it had been the practice to clear and plough up occasional crofts of marginal moorland, take a crop or two of oats and rye from it, then let it go back to moorland, for furze (gorse) was important for fuel. Until 1839 some farmers were actually sowing furze seeds, and large furze ricks were kept on farms for winter fuel. Since west Cornwall especially had been denuded of trees, it was only the increasing accessibility of Welsh coal that ended this practice.

The mechanization of agriculture began in 1812 with Richard Trevithick's steam threshing-machine; reaping-machines came in from 1852, throwing numbers of labourers out of work during a depression. Steam ploughs were tried, without success; not until tractors arrived in the twentieth century were horses replaced. Stall feeding of animals began about 1860 and increased as crops gave better yields due to imported fertilizers.

Before Carew's time Cornish sheep had produced such poor-quality wool, known as 'Cornish hair', that it had been exported without duty. But by the seventeenth century selective breeding had produced a healthy wool industry, as witness the many place-names such as Vellandruckya, Valley Truckle and Tuckingmill, up and down Cornwall, denoting places beside fast-flowing streams where the cloth was made or processed for use. The abolition of the Corn Laws in 1840 did not, as was feared, ruin Cornish farmers, who increased their investments in cattle and sheep. By 1880 Cornish farms carried nearly twice as many cattle per acre as the average for England and Wales, and a higher proportion of sheep and pigs also. Today, aided by combine harvesters, electric milking-machines, silos, tractors and so much other costly modern equipment, farms in Cornwall are among the most intensively worked.

The effect of the Common Market agricultural policy, however, reaches them from time to time. Restriction of milk production is now drastically reducing herds, and if over-production of milk, butter and cheese continues, there may well be a swing back to arable farming, as is indicated by the increasing number of oil-seed rape fields, now being sown in Cornwall, with their garish yellow carpets of flowers – the root is sold for margarine manufacture.

The early market garden industry has developed over the last 120 years, particularly in west Cornwall; it began when a steward on Harvey's packet took broccoli from Hayle to Bristol and sold it at a handsome profit. Spring cabbages and onions, carrots, lettuce, early potatoes and other produce were also soon marketed after the railway came west to Penzance, and today, most of it now being sent to London and other centres by heavy road transport, the trade is a lucrative and staple one, though from time to time frosts after Christmas decimate the crops. Many young plants are now grown under glass, and early tomatoes from greenhouses compete with Channel Island and imported produce.

The flourishing Scillonian flower industry, which markets daffodils and narcissi from November onwards, is now being followed by growers in the Mounts Bay area who successfully harvest crops of these flowers for January and February sales in the upcountry markets. The fruit-growing hillsides along the west bank of the River Tamar, where apples, pears and plums are grown, and the recent expansions of strawberry fields up and down the land (usually inviting one to 'Pick your own') are further indications of a diverse and, on the whole, prosperous horticulture, though the gradual

Calstock Viaduct

disappearance of the many Tamar Valley cherry orchards (due to ravages of birds) and cider orchards, over the past fifty years, is something many east Cornwall people bemoan.

Fishing has been one of the chief means of subsistence in Cornwall since neolithic times. Middle and New Stone Age hunters left shell middens and also the bones of hake, cod, ling and bass, indicating that they were not simply coastal fishermen. The ancient art of spear-fishing, which survived until recently in the Isles of Scilly, was plied inshore.

When nets came into use, probably in Celtic times, fish hauls increased, as did the human population. By Carew's time, the later sixteenth century, fishing activities were prolific: salmon and peal were taken in the rivers by hook, by tickling them from under the bank, by three-pronged salmon spear and by trapping in 'hutches' of stones built in the riverbeds. There were trout and other freshwater fish to be had, and oyster fisheries along the Lynher, Tamar and Helford estuaries and in Falmouth Haven. But the great fishing was pilchard seining, mainly then in the south-east and far west.

The same basic principle of seining continued until the last shoals were caught in this century: three or four boats to each great net (sometimes half a mile long), directed to shoot by a huer on the cliffs who shouted or signalled with his 'bush' – originally of furze, later of whitened canvas on hoops; trumpets were also used. The net being shot, the entrapped shoal was drawn into shallow water. In Carew's day the local populace came to buy on the beach direct from the fishermen, after which the main part of the catch would be bulked and pressed, the oil being extracted (it was used for lamps and other purposes); then it was salted and packed into barrels, and some was exported, for the immense Continental fish trade was beginning to expand. 'Fumadoes' – smoked pilchards – were also popular; others were split open and sun-dried.

Catholic fastdays encouraged the consumption of fish; there were at least ninety of them in each year. Tudor governments attempted, not very successfully, to encourage home sales of fish by discouraging exports, but by the late seventeenth century exports were rewarded by a bounty, though a tax on imported salt caused resentment and widespread smuggling. During the first half of that century Cornish fishermen had been plagued by marauding Dunkirkers and North African pirates; Fowey was said to be 'decayed in shipping' due to 'Turkish pirates' operating off shore. A strong Commonwealth Navy put an end to this situation, and fishing began to prosper again.

The pilchards, however, moved west, and soon Mount's Bay and West Cornwall were benefiting; the fish arrived later and sometimes stayed through the winter. Seining with larger boats and nets developed during the eighteenth century. Stop nets, brought across the mouths of the seine by a stop-boat, and tuck nets to empty out the haul, were introduced. These operations were financed mainly by merchants and landowners who built the fish-palaces or pent-houses for the processing of the catch and organized exports to France, Spain and Italy. At St Ives, however, the fishermen themselves shared everything in an early co-operative system.

From the mid eighteenth to late nineteenth century the vast shoals came; exports rose from around 15,000 hogsheads in the late seventeenth century to 30,000 in 1747–56, and 65,000 in 1796 (when there was insufficient salt to cure the whole catch), although lean years occurred at times. Since each hogshead held 3,000 fish or so, the 1796

RNLI station, Whitesand Bay, Sennen

figure represents nearly 200 million pilchards. There was a depression during the French Wars, but in 1827 there were 315 seines operating around Cornish coasts, employing 2,000 men at sea and 6,000 men, women and children on shore. In a single hour in November 1834 St Ives seines enclosed 10,000 hogshead (30 million fish). From Sennen in the west to Portwrinkle in the east and Port Isaac to the north, ports small and large participated. In 1877 there were 390 seines being worked.

But the last good seine year was 1907, with 8,000 hogsheads brought ashore at St Ives; the industry had been failing since the 1890s. Gradually the shoals deserted Cornish coasts, and though there is a cannery at Penzance today, pilchards comprise only a small proportion of fish taken.

Herring drifting or driving began in the early eighteenth century, when St Ives and Mount's Bay boats ventured into the Irish sea, as far up as Scotland; by the mid nineteenth century fleets of luggers from

Porthleven, Penzance, Newlyn, Mousehole and St Ives were sailing in the early months of the year to take advantage of the North Sea herring season. By March they would be home again for the mackerel season. This kind of fishing was very much subject to the vagaries of weather and supply of fish; 1839 was a particularly poor year. But the sight of the great fleets of drifters sailing from St Ives and Mount's Bay lingers in the memory, immortalized by evocative paintings and by photographs of late Victorian and Edwardian times.

The advent of East Coast fleets of steam trawlers and drifters, fishing in Cornish waters from November to March, began another era. Newlyn Harbour had been greatly enlarged; a new fish dock and shed were built at Padstow in 1910–12, and trainloads of mackerel, herring, skate, whiting, sole and other bottom-feeding fish were sent up daily to Billingsgate, a trade which lasted until 1939. Some ill-feeling grew between the Cornishmen and the newcomers; at Newlyn there was a riot because the East Coast crews fished on Sundays. Finally, unable to compete with the larger steam-powered craft, the St Ives and Mount's Bay fleets were sold off and broke up during the 1920s.

After 1950 Scottish trawler fleets joined the seasonal fishing, followed by large Brixham trawlers and Continentals with beam trawls and fine purse-seine nets, scouring the sea bed for all fish, small and large; much of their catch today is sold to Russian and East European factory ships lying off Falmouth during the winter. Fishing stocks began to be depleted, and quota systems have recently been imposed by the Ministry of Agriculture and Fisheries; two-monthly limits on catches of sole, plaice or mackerel, in force from time to time, are a beginning towards regulating affairs. Meanwhile the smaller Cornish boats, helped by loans and subsidies, equipped with echo sounders, radio, radar and powerful diesel engines, compete with the armada of foreign and British craft in their own waters. Some eighty boats work from Mevagissey, about twenty each from Newquay, Padstow and Looe. Twenty-four are based at Falmouth and 150 at Newlyn – which is now the third largest fishing port in the UK. In addition to the traditionally favoured fish, rock salmon or dogfish is increasingly caught and sold to Continental buyers; and the development of sea-water tanks in which to keep lobsters and crayfish, at Padstow and Newlyn, has boosted a prosperous trade supplying shellfish to hotels and restaurants in Britain and France.

After thousands of years at his trade, the Cornish fisherman is still in business, sometimes helped, sometimes hindered, by government and Common Market regulations. He will need all his traditional perseverance to continue into the twenty-first century, but there is ample hope that he will survive and even prosper.

Steam train at Padstow Station, about 1920

The growth of light industry in Cornwall over the years 1965–85 has added considerably to the well-being of the economy; indeed, taken with heavy industry already established (such as the production of mining equipment at Camborne and ship repairs at Falmouth), it is now the single largest contributor to Cornish earnings. On present figures these firms, mostly small, some branches of larger concerns, sell over £400 million worth of their products, exceeding agriculture (£375 million) and tourism (£250 million), both of which until now vied together as the major contributors. The arrival of these firms has been fairly consistently encouraged by government policies, backed by local authorities, to entice them from the large centres, particularly London, in order to aid peripheral areas.

These enterprises are far too numerous to detail here, and there is always a considerable percentage which, having obtained the loans or grants available and rented factory space provided, fail to thrive and move out again or go into liquidation. But a few examples of those well-established may suffice: colour printing near St Ives, chemicals at Bude and Tintagel, electronic equipment at Helston and Bodmin, computer software and biscuits at Truro, machine components at Wadebridge, paper products at Launceston, steel fabrications at Saltash, book-binding at Penryn and boat-building at Porthleven. A

Moorswater Industrial Estate, Liskeard

growing group of heavier industries produce building materials: granite blocks and paving slabs at Hayle, natural stone and grit-blasting at Launceston, scaffolding hire at St Austell. The various firms running fleets of heavy transport vehicles provide haulage for the china clay and other industries.

The building of new houses and flats, and the renovation and conversion of old buildings from barns and cottages to Victorian houses, chapels and warehouses, is a considerable industry in itself, refurbishing the face of town and country – not always creditably; though it must be said that, without this renovation, which is due mainly to people moving into Cornwall or buying seasonal homes, there would be an accelerating delay requiring massive grants and investments to correct.

The newcomers bring new attitudes and require social adjustments, as do incoming industries, but young Cornish people in this computerized and electronic age are now being provided with new types of work, and though the wage structure is not what one would wish, many are thus given a chance to remain in their native land.

9 Cottages, Farmhouses and Manors

The situation of Cornwall and its windswept, moist climate have caused its people down the ages to develop their own distinctive types of buildings in which to live, particularly farmhouses and cottages. Granite and slate, as might be expected, predominate as building-materials, but during the Dark and Middle Ages the practice of building in rubble stone – randomly acquired from any nearby source – was the most widely used by the well-to-do, surviving even today in some great houses like Cotehele. The lower stratas of society resorted to cob – a mixture of mud with small stones, straw and sometimes horsehair. Numerous town dwellings and country cottages, barns and farmbuildings have walls made in this unlikely material, which has lasted for hundreds of years.

Carew, describing in 1602 the materials to hand, long before the era of bricks, wrote:

> For walling there are the rough and the slate; the rough [rubble] maketh speedier building, the slate surer. For windows, dornes [door jambs] and chimneys, moor stone [granite] carrieth the chief reckoning. The name is bestowed on it by the moors or waste ground where the same is found in great quantity, either lying upon the ground or very little under. This stone . . . countervaileth its great hardness in the working with the profit of long endurance, nature having ordained the same, as of purpose, to withstand the fretting weather. There are also three other sorts of stones serving to the same use, and hewed with less though differing labour: Pentewan digged out of the sea cliffs, and in colour somewhat resembling grey marble; Caraclouse black, not unlike the jet; the third taken out of inland quarries, and not much differing from the eastern freestone.

One might quarrel a little with Carew's description of the dark blue-grey elvan from the Cataclewse quarry near Trevose Head, so well used in north Cornish churches, but his summary is admirable and as usual succinct. He realized, of course, the great advantages of using indigenous stone but must also have been aware of so much building in cob. Built up gradually, layer on layer, the mixture set hard, providing dwellings which were warm in winter and cool in summer; the thick walls kept the rain out well enough, but rising damp must always have been a problem. Generally cottages in medieval times were built by manorial tenant farmers for their workers; later in some areas miner-crofters were encouraged to build their own homes on land leased to them.

Most of the original Cornish cob cottages, apart from those in north Cornwall and on Bodmin Moor, were thatched; they were low-built – a single floor only, with perhaps a loft – and the eaves would come well down to protect the walls; where possible, they would be built into the lee of a hill slope for shelter. Some have rubble or even slate walls at one end, the weather side.

Very many of such cottages have, of course, been destroyed or rebuilt with newer materials. Today they are disappearing because modern building regulations make it difficult to improve them for twentieth-century habitation. Until recently it was prohibitively expensive and almost impossible to find thatchers to reroof them; there has now been a distinct revival of the thatching trade, and more money is available, mainly because of wealthier owners moving into Cornwall. Excellent examples of thatched Cornish cottages may be seen at Perranzabuloe, St Clement and Tresillian near Truro, St Keverne and the Lizard, and there is the celebrated Friends' meeting-house at Come-to-Good. A group of remarkable late thatched cottages are the Veryan round houses, erected by a Lostwithiel builder about 1820; they have Gothic Revival windows, one a porch, and remain almost exactly as they were built, standing at the approaches of this exquisite village.

The cottages of north and east Cornwall are built of cob or rubble, and naturally enough slate roofs have been traditional for centuries. Often lichened and grouted, they blend unobtrusively into the countryside. The typical miner's cottage of west Cornwall, slate-roofed and made of freestone and moorstone, with the latter providing corners and sills, presents a solid four-square and unpretentious, wholly natural dwelling. Whole streets of them, extensions of the natural landscape into the towns, can be seen in Camborne, Redruth, St Day, Troon, Illogan, St Agnes, Praze-an-Beeble and other villages.

The almshouses of Cornwall are a particularly fascinating study. The legacy of various benefactors, mainly landowners who after the

An eighteenth-century farm labourer's cottage:
Roaring Stiles, St Keverne

Stone cottages at Crugmeer near Padstow

Reformation saw that the elderly poor needed privacy combined with care, they are an enduring expression of benevolent patronage. The Moyle almshouses at St Germans are the earliest (late sixteenth century): constructed on two levels, with slate-hung gable ends brought forward over a shared balcony above a loggia. They thus provide twelve flats; renovated in 1967, they once more serve their original purpose. Near the church at Fowey are the seventeenth-century Rashleigh almshouses, and at Tregony a series of six, somewhat in the manner of St Germans. At Par a charming little row of seven, looking like dolls' houses, have also recently been restored and occupied. At Paul above Mousehole is the well-preserved early eighteenth-century Hutchins group. The tradition of providing for the worthy poor went on into the nineteenth century, saving many a respectable indigent from the workhouse; at Padstow the Tredwen almshouses, hidden away in the centre of the old town, were built in

1878; they are of Victorian red brick, however, and squeezed in each side of a rather claustrophobic cobbled court behind a narrow, arched gateway.

The development of Cornish farmhouses and small manor houses is an involved story, and one which cannot be documented in great detail here; the recommended book on the subject is *The Cornishman's House*, by F. J. and V. M. Chesher. The origin of these houses can be traced back to the Dark Age and medieval long houses, a type still found in Scotland (the *Ti Du*, 'black house') and the ancient farmhouses of Brittany.

In Cornwall their ancestry goes back at least to the small houses of this type excavated in 1950–54 in the sands at Mawgan Porth near Newquay; they date from the ninth or tenth century. These long houses were built of rubble stone, in two courses, filled between with clay soil and shillet. This has been the method of construction of Cornish hedges down to the present day; several farmhouses still retain parts built thus, one being Pengenna in St Kew, which actually has three storeys. The Mawgan Porth houses were all grouped around a central courtyard – which seems to be a development of the system used at Chysauster, Carn Euny and other Iron Age courtyard house groups. Each long house itself was basically one large room without ceilings, possessing only a rough loft reached by a ladder, and a second smaller room adjoining it; the humans' living, eating and sleeping quarters were in the main long room, where there was a hearth, and cattle or pigs were housed in the secondary room. This arrangement persisted well into medieval times in the poorer farmhouses; beaten earth floors were usual, though later slate flags were put down. Farmhouses of this type have been excavated or examined at Lanyon in Morvah and at Garrow Tor on Bodmin Moor.

Later versions of the long house had upper floors put in and stone stairs added on by means of a projection or turret: Trewitten and Treforda, both near Boscastle, are good instances. Indeed, as time went on and the Great Rebuild got underway, nearly all the larger houses in both towns and country were drastically altered and enlarged, often by raising their roofs to accommodate an upper floor and sometimes by the addition of wings. Cross-passages had come in, with moulded main doorways; porches were added, often with rooms built above them. The house was now divided into the gentry's quarters – the large hall, often left open up to the roof, the parlour and bedrooms; and the servants' quarters on the other side of the cross-passage, where were the kitchen, buttery and dairy. Byres and stables were built outside and often grouped around a courtyard, forming the 'town place'. In addition to stair projections, chimneys were added, either on one end of the house, especially in the case of

Slate cottages at Boscastle

kitchens, or laterally, to serve the great fireplace needed to warm the main hall. The best and most accessible example is that of the Old Post Office, Tintagel, a fine slate-built medieval manor house, now in the hands of the National Trust and open to the public; the various extensions from the original can be clearly detected. Ogbeare Hall,

North Tamerton, is partly fifteenth century and worthy of study.

Gables were a common feature added during the sixteenth and seventeenth centuries, usually as a result of building rooms into the roof space; Tintagel Old Post Office and other old houses at Bossinney are outstanding in this respect. The parlour was the room which denoted one's aspirations to a more genteel life; many farmhouses divided off a parlour from the hall, building bedrooms above it; others added one as part of a new wing. Roskruge Barton, St Anthony in Meneage, has such a wing added on at right angles to the old house. Later, towards the end of the seventeenth century, two-storey houses were being built, often with a room over the porch – as at the lovely battlemented house at Tresungers in St Endellion.

Often manor houses of Elizabethan times were planned around a courtyard, as at Roscarrack in north Cornwall, Trevear, St Stephen-in-Brannel, and Trenethick Barton, Wendron. At Lanooe in St Kew are the remnants, with Tudor and later additions, of a medieval farm complex (it was originally the Celtic monastery of St Docco), which had grown into a small village; a remarkable survival. Many delightful small Tudor mullioned windows are preserved in these houses of the Great Rebuild: among them Welltown in Forrabury, Trevear, Mudgeon in Mullion and Trevollard at St Veep come to mind. None of these is easily found, being at the end of lanes off the main roads, but all are well worth the effort of travelling to see.

During the late seventeenth and eighteenth centuries Cornwall became more open to outside influence, as will be seen by the considerable number of William and Mary, Georgian and Regency buildings up and down the Duchy. A number of farmhouses were built in the manner of larger mansions – the square sashed windows, hipped roofs and more severe lines can be plainly seen in those at Rosecadghill, Penzance (about 1695) and continuing with Rosmeryn, St Budock and Angrouse, near Mullion, both later eighteenth century. Trengoffe in Warleggan and Tregirls near Padstow (early nineteenth century) are spacious examples built for gentlemen farmers.

Parsonages may be coupled with farmhouses, since for several centuries, indeed well into Victorian times, the rector or vicar was often himself an active farmer, exploiting to the full his glebe land. The rise in social esteem achieved by incumbents in the eighteenth century resulted in previous small and inadequate parsonages being destroyed or rebuilt or acquiring grander Georgian fronts. The latter happened at Sithney, which shows clearly the previous building, including an earlier wing and a linhay. At Padstow the vicarage was pulled down and an imposing new one built in its own grounds half a mile away. At Morwenstow about 1840 the Reverend R. S. Hawker built his egregious vicarage, with its chimneys modelled on church towers he and his family had been associated with, and farmed his glebe land from it.

The large manor houses and mansions of the county families loom upon the landscape, self-evidently important; some are now in the hands of the National Trust and open during most of the year. Others, still in private hands, admit the public on certain days, mainly to show their houses and exotic gardens in support of charities. A new group, which has recently had the assistance of the Historic Buildings Trust in order to carry out necessary repairs and renovations, will henceforth as a result of agreements with the Department of the Environment be admitting the public; Prideaux Place, Padstow, and Harlyn House, three miles further west, are among them. It is not possible to cover all these great houses in detail here, for in every district if not parish there is at least one large historic house set in well-planned grounds.

Their building was the result of increasing wealth among landed families, beginning as far back as the original houses at Cotehele and Pengersick in the fourteenth century; the produce of the land, wool and tin and, in some cases, the reward of services to the Crown laid the foundations of their building, especially after the Reformation when the well-to-do no longer channelled as much of their income into the church. Later, merchants and mining adventurers built their mansions, in several cases earning or buying titles to go with them.

Pengersick Castle is now but a rump of what it used to be: a three-storeyed castellated wing of the original with square turret attached, its medieval hall house with porch was in ruins in the eighteenth century, and for some time it was used as a barn. The Georgian farmhouse near it has a doorway from the hall. It was the most important house in the district and dominated the slope of land down to Praa Sands and Mounts Bay. As it decayed, a series of local legends of the Lord or Enchanter of Pengersick grew up, based on murders and other scandalous involvements of the Pengersick and Milliton families who had lived there; these provided much material for William Bottrell and Robert Hunt.

Cotehele Manor above the Tamar also has a superb position, its gardens with ponds and dovecote descending in a valley to the river; the first house of the Edgcumbe family, it contains much sixteenth-century work. It is built around a series of courts, on a scale which is not at all formidable; the main parts were built by Sir Richard

Trevollard, St Veep

Cotehele House (the dining room)

Edgcumbe, who died in 1489, and Sir Piers, who died in 1539. Richard Edgcumbe's gatehouse, with its square imposing tower made of cut granite blocks, rises above an original fourteenth-century rubble wall on the south side. The great hall is Piers' work and is justly celebrated; the chapel is late sixteenth century. Bacchic tapestries enliven the Punch Room; they are probably Soho work, about 1700. The Edgcumbes built their great new house, Mount Edgcumbe, overlooking Plymouth Sound, during 1547–54; it had four corner towers and a hall rising higher above them but was bombed during the Second World War and, though restored in 1960, is now of little architectural interest. The gardens, however, are magnificent in their scope and, now jointly owned by Plymouth City and Cornwall County Council, are open throughout the year and well patronized, especially by Plymouthians. They include English, French and Italian formal gardens, various monuments, two temples and an imitation ruin folly.

Harlyn House, soon to be opened to the public, has a Georgian front behind which there is an earlier house, a medieval dovecote and outbuildings going back to Tudor times and before; it may have been a small monastic establishment in the Middle Ages. It has a fine late Norman doorway which may well have come from the ruined church at Constantine below the house.

At Rialton in the valley behind St Columb Minor is the main wing of Prior Vivian's manor house: late fifteenth century, with a large battlemented porch containing three long mullioned windows with round heads; this great upper room is said to have been the prior's study when he was in retreat from his affairs at Bodmin. The delightful setting and the proud house can be viewed from the road above it, which leads to Newquay.

Erth Barton, near Saltash, also has a fine porch and some graceful mullioned windows; it was built in the late sixteenth century, but the fourteenth-century chapel remains, though used as a barn; in it are, or were, remains of wall paintings and a medieval arch.

Arwennack House at Falmouth was largely destroyed during the Civil War, but some Elizabethan work remains; the chapel and hall, its best features, have disappeared. It was the manor of the Killigrew family who promoted Falmouth as a borough; an obelisk to them stands opposite the house site, above the foreshore. Trecarrel, near Launceston, is also a mere shadow of what it ought to be; its builder, Sir Henry Trecarrel, abandoned it half-built on the death of his wife and turned his attention and his wealth to the rebuilding of St Mary Magdalene's Church in Launceston, for which we may well be thankful. However, Trecarrel's magnificent hall remains, once used as a barn but now restored, and also his chapel; they are among Cornwall's most valuable early sixteenth-century heritages.

Trerice, near Newquay, now a National Trust property, is one of the most perfect Elizabethan mansions in Cornwall; it was the home of the Catholic Arundells, who suffered so much for their faith under Edward and Elizabeth. The hall, like that of Cotehele, is open to the roof and has an immense latticed window; stairs from it lead to a solar room of later period, beautifully displaying Brussels tapestries of about 1530. There is also much excellent late sixteenth-century plasterwork. Trerice was the home of the fifth Sir John Arundell, son of the Sir John who built the main part of the house we have today; he held Pendennis Castle for the King in a heroic five-month siege in 1646, when he was seventy years of age.

Stanbury near Morwenstow, in the extreme north of Cornwall, is a charming Elizabethan house of 1585, L-shaped, with a great hall and a two-storeyed porch. Not far from it is the more modest manor house of Tonacombe, of the same period.

Trerice House

The Prideaux ('Priddow') family have been at Padstow since the mid sixteenth century; as a result of acquiring their land from the Crown when Elizabeth I sold off so much of what her father, Henry, had seized, they were able to build Prideaux Place above the town, where they remain. Much of the east front of their house is of 1570 and just after, but later additions were made, particularly in the eighteenth century when the library and bow-windowed parlour were added. Superb biblical scenes carved in plaster can be seen on the ceiling of what used to be the Great Chamber, above the hall.

Another branch of the Prideaux family built Prideaux ('Priddux') House near Luxulyan, one early sixteenth-century wing of which survives, recently renovated, with its porch and three-light windows. The Rashleighs acquired it and later built the Georgian house below it. Lanherne (St Mawgan in Pydar), since 1794 the home of Carmelite nuns, is basically Tudor; it was an Arundell house and still retains its Elizabethan front. There are some interesting and elaborate Cornish crosses in its grounds; the convent chapel is open to the public. Exquisitely situated above this quiet, tree-shrouded village, it is a haven of peace juxtaposed ironically with St Mawgan Aerodrome less than half a mile away.

Morval House, inland from Looe, was originally an E-shaped Tudor building, adjoining the church. It was re-roofed in the eighteenth century and lost its central porch but remains a manor of considerable charm, hidden away off the bend of the main road. Not far from it at Pelynt is Trelawne, the house of the famous Trelawnys; Sir Jonathan bought the house and estate from Elizabeth I. It contains a late thirteenth-century turret, and parts of the fifteenth-century chapel were incorporated into the present nineteenth century building; the Trelawnys became Catholic in that century.

Heligan, near Pentewan, is one of the earliest seventeenth-century Cornish houses, with an unfussy front of six bays, although most of the work seen now is later rebuilding. The gardens are a great delight. The house has now been converted into residential flats.

Ince Castle (probably early seventeenth century, perhaps earlier) was one of the first houses in Cornwall to be built of brick; constructed on a square plan, it has no main hall or staircase. The later addition of slate hangings on its towers has softened the effect and blended it well into the landscape; the former tower battlements have given place to pyramid-shaped roofs, which gives an original effect, rather like viewing a romantic faery palace from across the river. The influence of French *châteaux* may be responsible.

Lanhydrock, the greatest manor in Cornwall, with some of the most extensive grounds, including a lovely avenue of beeches leading to the magnificent gatehouse, was begun about 1620 by Sir Richard Roberts, a Truro tin and wool magnate who became Lord Robartes – he is said to have paid £10,000 for his title. The glory of the house is its long gallery, today used for concerts organized by the National Trust, in whose care the estate is; the ceiling is covered with biblical figures carved in plaster – probably by the same north Devon craftsmen whose work is seen at Prideaux Place. They include a lissom Adam and Eve being banished from the Garden of Eden by an athletic archangel, and Judas administering his kiss to Christ. Portraits of the Robartes family down the centuries stare lugubriously at one from the walls. The gardens are full of well-tended exotic plants, with a formal rose-garden on the north side of the house; also in the grounds is the little church of St Hydroc, which was a family chapel. In 1888 the great house was devastated by fire (a common enough occurrence, as it appears, in the days of oil lamps, roaring log fires and bed-warmers), and it was rebuilt in more or less the same manner, with some additions. It is a great attraction to visitors and produces immense revenues for the Trust.

In east Cornwall is Penheale, a large manor house begun about the

Lanhydrock House (the Long Gallery)

same time as Lanhydrock; it also has its gatehouse, rows of fine mullioned windows and an elaborate screen of 1640 in its hall. A wing was added in the eighteenth century, and in the early twentieth century Sir Edward Lutyens, architect of Castle Drogo in Devon, built a tower-like addition of four storeys with stone-mullioned windows, a bold if hardly suitable venture which almost blends in with the rest.

Trewen Hall outside St Columb was begun about 1633, though much of it, including the Gothic windows, is nineteenth-century work. A fine battlemented H-shaped house with projecting wings, on a hilltop screened by great trees, it is now a holiday centre.

Stow Barton is all that remains of the great seventeenth-century Grenville House which was pulled down in the eighteenth century, as a result of family losses, perhaps over the South Sea Bubble or a similar venture. Parts of the huge house were sold off and incorporated into other mansions. With eleven bays it was by far the largest Cornish house of its kind. The farm is a distinctive building in its own right, incorporating the former stables.

Trelowarren, six miles from Helston, is an intriguing mixture of periods, though happily not of contrasting styles. The east wing has a good deal of the fifteenth century; the polygonal bay window on the south is 1662; the stables are 1698; the chapel and battlements are mid eighteenth century, and the north wing is early Victorian. Yet it presents a wholesome unity, set among its acres of trees and lawns. It was the home of the Vyvyan family, who were great Royalists during the Civil War. They later built the charming neo-Gothick thatched lodges at the entrance of their drive; they are similar in type and period to the Veryan round houses. Trelowarren House is now used for seminars and music studies, and its great Tudor barn as a craft centre.

Battlements or crenellations, though merely decorations, were well in favour during the seventeenth century; Penrose, overlooking Loe Pool near Helston, has an embattled front of this period, though the rest of it is later. Tregarden in St Mabyn is an excellently proportioned house of 1631 with small mullioned windows and a most inviting quadrangle behind its granite gateposts. Marhays near Marhamchurch is mainly of the same age, despite a surviving fourteenth-century doorway; there are some ornately carved plaster ceilings inside.

Bochym Manor, south of Helston, though since greatly added to and rebuilt, retains late seventeenth-century parts and is something of an eccentric among buildings of its period. There are three gabled bays and a castellated clocktower, and the mullions are much wider than those of previous houses. It is now a holiday establishment.

Again near Helston, Godolphin House is justly celebrated: it reveals perhaps the earliest neo-Classical influence in Cornish building, with loggia and elegant Tuscan columns along its north side. The Godolphin family were involved in state affairs from the reign of Henry VIII onwards and were staunch Royalists during the Civil

War; Sidney Godolphin rose to become Lord Treasurer (in effect Prime Minister) under Queen Anne. The mullioned windows above the columns were thought by Pevsner to be mid seventeenth century work, which if correct would date the whole front. In its secluded woodland setting, with box hedges and a serene, slightly decayed air, it radiates a lingering sense of former importance and grandeur.

The William and Mary era, already producing many new Classically styled houses in England, did not affect Cornwall greatly, but the four square mansion Sir William Coryton built between 1685 and 1695 at Newton Ferrers above the River Lynher in south-east Cornwall was certainly the first, having no survival of earlier styles. Unfortunately, most of it was destroyed by fire, though some of it has since been rebuilt. A similar mansion at Croan, between Wadebridge and Bodmin on the hillbrow above the River Laine or Allen, was erected a few years later for a successful lawyer who set himself up as squire; it uses granite and local freestone to solid and attractive effect. Roscadghill House on the outskirts of Penzance was built in the same style for the Borlase family (who obviously had upcountry associations) in 1690.

These Classical houses, with large, square-paned windows, often with pillared porches and pediments, began to preside over the Cornish landscape in some strength during the early eighteenth century and signalled in manor-house building what is often referred to as 'the Death of the Vernacular' (though some later mansions, especially in Victorian times, incorporated distinctively Cornish features). Notable among these new houses are Shillingham on the north bank of the Lynher (1700), Antony House on the south side (1710–25), Trewithen near Probus (1715–40, with two brick wings), Boconnoc near Lostwithiel (1720 onwards), Trereiffe near Penzance, Ethy above Lerryn, Menabilly (1710–15) near Fowey and Castle Horneck (1720) outside Penzance. Antony is the grandest of them, replacing an earlier Carew house in which the celebrated historian Richard wrote his *Survey*. It is mainly of Pentewan stone, with nine handsome bays, and looks down between avenues of trees to the pacific river. Inside is an excellent collection of Queen Anne furniture.

Of the mid eighteenth century, Acton Castle near Perranuthnoe is a small mansion with battlements, principally of granite, though it has modern wings. At the other end of Cornwall, Moditonham House in Botus Fleming is larger, with seven bays, three storeys and a nice Doric porch; it was built on or near the site of a Norman castle owned by the Moditon family. Treworgey near Liskeard also has seven bays and a Tuscan porch; its gardens are well known for their sculptured yews, and a weatherboard clock tower with Chinese roof

Boconnoc House

adds a touch of whimsical exoticism. The house is mainly seventeenth century, refaced in the Georgian style.

Ebbingford Manor near Bude has fourteenth-century doorways but was restored in 1758, though retaining its mullioned windows; in summer it is open to the public, with craft shops and gifts. Some eighteenth-century houses have been hung with slate and are thereby rendered less formal and fit more naturally into the Cornish landscape; Glebe House (the Old Rectory) at Philleigh above the River Fal is one such, and lords over the surrounding thatched cottages and pub.

One of the great Georgian houses of Cornwall is Pencarrow near Bodmin (1765–78), seated behind deep rhododendron-lined drives and a plantation of venerable trees from many climes; its south face looks onto a circular pool with fountain, amid well-kept lawns. It has seven bays, of 2½ storeys, with attractive pediments over the first-floor windows. It belongs to the Molesworth family and is now open most days during the summer. The music room with its Rococo ceiling is a gem. This was the home of Sir William Molesworth (1810–55), who was prominent in Parliament as a campaigner against transportation, which he helped to end, and as an advocate of free trade.

Tehidy House, outside Redruth, no longer exists as such; the last mansion there was gutted by fire in 1919 and has been replaced by a hospital. However, the stables, with cupola, and the four square pavilions, one (previously the chapel) with a clocktower, remain. The Georgian house of 1734 replaced other, earlier houses of the Basset family – they had been there since early Norman times. The expansion of copper-mining, especially the driving of the Pool Adit, financed the building; Portland and Bath stone was brought in, to be used along with local granite and freestone. This magnificent house, by Thomas Edwards of Greenwich, was later rebuilt at immense cost during the 1860s. The landscaped gardens included a lake and a temple (pulled down in 1808) made of locally fired bricks.

Carclew, south of Truro, was also partly by Thomas Edwards – it was generally agreed to be the most distinctive of Cornish Georgian houses. Sadly it too was burned out, in 1934. It had been the seat of the Lemon family, who built much of Truro and represented the

St Michael's Mount

town in Parliament. Calenick, a mile or two away, was built a decade later for a smelting 'captain', with a slate-hung upper storey and a 1752 clocktower.

These square-windowed Classical-type houses were still being built well into the nineteenth century: Glynn House, overlooking the middle Fowey valley near Bodmin, was rebuilt in 1805 with a large Ionic portico – a large house of nine bays, it now houses scientific laboratories. There are also Killiowe in Kea (about 1790, added to in 1850) which is now part of a country park enterprise; Pentillie Castle (1810–15, demolished in 1968, although a seventeenth-century wing remains); Sconner House near Sheviock, with an impressive pillared entrance hall, stuccoed and Regency; Clowance in Crowan, formerly a home of the St Aubyn family, who own St Michael's Mount; and Penrice near St Austell, now a home for the elderly. Within the Norman castle at Trematon, near Saltash, a Georgian house was built and part of the bailey wall taken down to give it a view down to the Plymouth Sound.

Port Eliot, almost adjoining the great Norman church at St Germans, came into the Eliot family in 1565; it was originally a priory, but very little of that survives beyond some thirteenth-century lancet windows and the refectory, which is now the hall. Sir John Eliot MP was famous for his championship of Parliamentary rights and died in the Tower of London in 1632, imprisoned for his beliefs by Charles I. For this treatment the Eliot family later received £5,000 as compensation. The present house with its Georgian windows and castellations is largely the work of Sir John Sloane, between 1802 and 1806. There is a grand 'Tudor Gothic' porch of 1843 which reflects the style of the twin gatehouses of the same date. The park was laid out by Sir Humphrey Repton in 1792 and contains rolling lawns and the obligatory lake of its era. In July of each year the Elephant Fayre is held in the grounds, attracting numerous stalls, amusements *avant-garde* and esoteric, and many hundreds of washed and unwashed young people involved in various alternative life-styles. The fair's name comes from the Eliot family crest, which depicts an elephant's head.

Trelissick House, set above the west bank of the Fal at King Harry Passage, possesses sweeping vistas downriver; it is a plain Georgian building remarkable mainly for its tremendous Ionic portico, by P. F. Robinson (1825): six columns and pediment rising to the roof, and well out of scale with the house itself. The beautifully planned gardens are in the care of the National Trust; also in the grounds is Lys Escop, the residence of the Bishop of Truro.

Caerhayes Castle (1808) on the south coast is an ambitious yet remarkably unobtrusive castellated Georgian house, with gardens

Trelissick House

landscaped into terraces against a background of trees, many of them ornamental and exotic. It was the work of John Nash (architect of Buckingham Palace) and has a square turret on the west end and a round one on the east.

Restormel House, built below Restormel Castle but above the banks of the Fowey near Lostwithiel, was the first Gothic Revival house in Cornwall; it was built in the 1760s, battlemented, and does its best to look like a little medieval castle. Tregenna Castle, later a hotel, at St Ives, is a similar edifice, built in 1774 and designed by Wood of Bath; it has been considerably extended since. A variety of styles came into use for the construction of large houses during the nineteenth century. Tregothnan House, seat of the earls of Falmouth, above the east bank of the Tresillian river, is in a style known as East Anglian Tudor; its stone-framed windows have no mullions but there are small balconies and a proliferation of tall, unsightly chimneys; it must be, after Lanhydrock, the largest Cornish mansion. It is mainly the work of William Wilkins (1816–18) and Lewis Vulliamy (1845–87). The grounds are open to the public on one or two days each year; its gardens and deerpark give expansive views down the green tree-lined highway of water.

Place, at St Anthony in Roseland, also has an enviable setting, looking across the Percueil river mouth to St Mawes; it contains remnants of the former priory and is still joined to the Norman cruciform church. Pevsner calls the house 'symmetrical neo-Gothic

Tregothnan House

at its least attractive', but this is perhaps a harsh judgement. The manor was the home of the Spry family for centuries; one of them, Thomas, attained the rank of admiral at the end of the seventeenth century, having fought under Rodney and Hood.

Place House, Fowey, as seen today, owes a great deal to the grandiloquent vision of Joseph Thomas Austin, who was born into the Treffry family and adopted their name; the owner of mines and quarries and builder of Par Harbour and the marvellous viaduct across the Luxulyan valley evidently wanted a house suitable for one who was unofficially known as 'the King of Mid Cornwall'. The work, in Romantic Gothic, went on from 1813 to 1845; fortunately, the exquisite sixteenth-century bay window was retained. As a young lad Neville Burnard was employed in stone carving on the new south bay; his bust of Treffry, executed years later, is inside the house.

St Michael's Mount, of all Cornish houses, has the most famous and unique setting; no one who has climbed up its stairways to inspect the various rooms and gaze out across Mount's Bay, with the sea washing the rocks far below, is likely to forget the experience. Thought to be the Ictis of classical tradition, where Phoenicians came to trade for tin, and in Cornish folklore the home of the giant Cormoran who sent his wife to get rocks from the Penwith moors to build the castle, it is more than romantic: it is a living accretion of history, containing as it does parts of the Benedictine monastic buildings of the twelfth century, among much later work. The former refectory is now the Chevy Chase Room; its ceiling is probably fifteenth century, and it has a remarkable plaster frieze depicting hunting scenes of various kinds. Under Sir John St Aubyn (died 1744) the Lady Chapel became the drawing-room and boudoir. Much of the later building is by J. P. St Aubyn, the architect member of the family who restored in such drastic and unfeeling fashion so many Cornish churches; here, however, he has produced excellent work in the south-east wing. There are several medieval crosses on the slopes below the house, which since the end of the last century have been planted with many fine exotic trees and shrubs.

Tresco Abbey on the Isles of Scilly is mainly the mid nineteenth-century work of the Lord Proprietor, Augustus Smith, who did so much to improve the economy of the islands, including encouraging the early daffodil trade. Two arches and some thirteenth-century walls of the Benedictine priory remain; there is an inscribed stone of the sixth century built into them. The house stands in the sub-tropical gardens which include the famous Valhalla, a colourful and well-preserved collection of ships' figureheads taken from wrecks around the Scillies.

The work of G. E. Street is evident at several places in Cornwall and is always worth inspecting. His St Faith's (now renamed Collamere) outside Lostwithiel above the Liskeard road, built as a convent but now a rest home, is of grey sandstone and dark Cornish slate; the centre three-storeyed block with buttresses and gables presents an effect of severe Victoriana, contrasting with the soft greenery of the hills and woods about it. In 1855 at St Columb, Street designed the Old Rectory which was rebuilt inside its moat in a solid neo-Elizabethan style, with large, gloomy rooms and dark, panelled parlours; it is now a restaurant and hotel.

Set back amid tree-filled grounds in the middle of St Austell is Polcarne House, in Victorian Italianate style of about 1860. An intriguing building by Alfred Waterhouse is the Crag, Maenporth, also now an hotel, built in 1865 into the steep cliff slope above the beach. It has granite pillars and uses mainly Cornish stone. Pencalenick House, east of Truro, was built in 1881 to the plans of J. P. St Aubyn, in a neo-Regency style; its quiet setting off the main roads enhances its solid presence.

Few houses of the manorial type or scale have been erected in the present century; among the most noteworthy is Daymer House, in the lee of Brea Hill, Trebetherick, on the Camel estuary. The work of A. Allen, 1910, it is a slate-hung, hipped-roofed building with seven bays, slate chimneys and pillars, set before a screen of brooding pines. A green of St Enodoc golf course lies just beyond its lawn. Trenowth near Grampound was built in 1928 in neo-Georgian style; below it are the remnants of a late medieval chapel.

Cornish town houses are many and varied, but few have survived from the late medieval period or earlier. Probably the earliest extant is Abbey House on the North Quay at Padstow, though that name was adopted only in the nineteenth century. It was a monastic building, probably the harbour toll house for the priory of Bodmin, though a school of thought believes it was also the guild house. Features such as the Cataclewse stone windows and the decorative heads may have come from a chapel known to have stood formerly almost adjacent to it. It is built on three storeys, with a turning flight of slate steps leading to a porch on the first floor, and rooms under them which until 1940 were used as net cellars.

At Mousehole a much admired building is Keigwin House, an inn during the eighteenth and nineteenth centuries but actually an Elizabethan or earlier manor house: with its porch on granite columns and room over, it takes quiet precedence in a narrow street over the later buildings around it. Stuart House in Liskeard is reputed to have been built in the first part of the sixteenth century by Sir Henry

LENNON

Trecarrel but is mainly later work, though some early Tudor granite features are incorporated into this large and venerable building.

Standing in wide Coinagehall Street in Helston is the Angel Hotel, originally the town house of the Godolphin family; some of it is Tudor work, including an assembly room with minstrel's gallery. This pleasant old inn with its dark beams and panelling, its unimproved but comfortable atmosphere of a former coaching inn (which it was), is a popular haunt for tourists as well as locals.

Dockacre House, Launceston, is late sixteenth century: low and long, with slated gables, it makes an interesting contrast with the mainly Georgian later buildings of the town. At Padstow St Petroc's House (now divided into flats) has a fine Queen Anne front with portico, concealing behind it an earlier L-shaped house, the home of town merchants since the late sixteenth century.

At the White Hart Inn at Launceston the coaching yard was glassed over, and bars and a restaurant have been built under this dome; the doorway with its colonnettes, said to be from the former priory of St Thomas (though Charles Henderson thought it might have come from the chapel of Launceston Castle), adds a venerable elegance.

The White Hart Hotel at St Austell is mainly Georgian, with some nice interior touches; it has some excellent modern paintings of the china clay district by John Nash RA. At Liskeard is Webb's Hotel, with a Tuscan porch before a square building of three storeys; it was by Foulston of Plymouth, who built a number of Regency-style houses in the town. The whole Parade of Liskeard, with its town hall and its stucco and slate-hung houses, is a harmonious achievement. Launceston also has a collection of fine Georgian and Regency residences, mainly on Castle Hill; the red brick Eagle House, with its dramatic bronze bird statues, is now an hotel. Marlborough House at Falmouth is one of the most distinctive buildings of the period, with a semicircular Doric porch of six columns; the town has a number of important Georgian and Regency houses, including the distinctive Custom House, with its impressive columned portico.

At Penzance, Regent Terrace and Square and Clarence Place and Terrace stand overlooking Mount's Bay on the west side of the town amid palms and flowering shrubs; other Georgian and early Victorian façades can be seen, mainly above shops in Market Jew Street. Penryn also possesses some former merchant's mansions, faced with granite ashlar, and a view of many of them from the back shows how the earlier buildings were extended with staircases, lateral chimneys, etc. An excellently proportioned nineteenth-century coaching inn,

Abbey House, Padstow

Launceston: town and castle

the Molesworth Arms at Wadebridge, has a pillared Tuscan porch, some good oak panelling and staircase; the former stable wings at the back have now been converted to extra bars, a dining-room and holiday flats.

But the supreme expression of the Georgian and Regency eras in Cornwall must be Truro, with its spacious mansions in Prince's Street. The Parade in Malpas Road, Benson House in Moresk Road (early eighteenth century) and Trehaverne House in Kenwyn Street continued the tradition of fine Classical houses into the outer parts of the city. Lemon Street, descending from Lander's Column with stately granite-faced terraced houses (now mainly offices) was one of the marvels of Cornwall, and justly famous. Whilst touring in 1811, Charles Dibden was told in Tavistock that, 'If he should have the happiness of seeing Truro, he should die contented.' Today's re-development of the main shopping areas of the city, however, would hardly produce such hyperbole.

The architecture and history of Cornish hotel building has not been by any means a wholly creditable story. Now that tourism has assumed such a permanent feature of life in Cornwall, it is surely high time that some attempt at a critique should be made; here only a few comments can be given. Where hotels have been adapted from existing buildings, such as the Tregenna Castle at St Ives or the Eagle Hotel at Launceston, or grown from coaching inns like the Red Lion at St Columb and Tyacke's Hotel at Camborne, the results are almost invariably pleasing and in good taste. Many, like the Georgian Royal Hotel at Truro and the Molesworth Arms, Wadebridge, have retained their classical fronts whilst redeveloping their stables and accommodation at the rear. The Penventon Hotel at Redruth, set well back in its own tree-filled grounds, was formerly a genteel residence, built in later Victorian times; the original front has been retained, with its stucco effect and pillared porch. Excellent adaptations to inns with accommodation have been made at the slate-built Old Mill, Treknow, in the Trebarwith valley, at Sladesbridge, near Wadebridge, and on the quayside at Padstow (the Old Custom House Inn).

Elsewhere, however, hotels designed as hotels have not been so aesthetically pleasing. The Edwardian mansion-like King Arthur's Castle Hotel at Tintagel, blocking a large slice of the sea view, is little short of disastrous; the Headland Hotel at Newquay, by Sylvanus Trevail of Truro, is an odd red-brick construction with pavilion roofs, creating a tiredly Oriental effect on one of the best sites in all Cornwall. The heavy and sombre Metropole Hotel at Padstow, built before the railway arrived there in 1899, hogs another prime piece of landscape, though it is mercifully partly concealed by pine trees. Some of the hotels at Newquay are individually pleasant enough: the Great Western, the Kilbirnie and the Edgcumbe may be mentioned. Above the town on Mount Wise, hotels from the 1930s onward appear, some like the Windsor with glassed fronts, but they do not obtrude. At Penzance some acceptable Edwardian hotels along the Esplanade fit in well with their surroundings. Portwrinkle in the extreme south-west has the dour mid-Victorian limestone Whitesand Bay Hotel, which was rebuilt in 1911 overlooking the long, curving strand; it was originally a manor house at Torpoint and was taken down and moved stone by stone.

There is indeed so much that is rewarding of study in all the towns and villages of Cornwall: slate-hung houses of various eras, Tudor cottages, Stuart farmhouses, Georgian mansions, stuccoed Regency terraces, three-storeyed Victorian houses, old warehouses, mills and

Walsingham Place, Truro

chapels refurbished for modern use. There are also many new developments, today sometimes slate-fronted at the insistence of planners – for instance, harmonious arcades of shops at Truro and Padstow, which, however, have regrettably replaced old traditional dwellings. The vernacular in Cornish house-building has returned to some extent since 1960, with attractive new stone-faced cottages (some of them council homes for senior citizens) – here again Padstow has some of the best examples. But in the rush to encourage council-house building in the 1950s and 60s an unrepeatable opportunity was lost to create distinctively Cornish-looking homes for the people who most of all should have had them to live in; the requisite vision was lacking at County Hall and on the district and urban councils. True, the not unattractive Cornish unit house, half-tiled in most cases (slates being considered too expensive) and utilizing blocks made from china clay sand, went up on housing estates all over the Duchy, but in far too many instances low-cost building schemes encouraged unimaginatively designed houses or dreary blocks of flats.

And the legacy of the jerry-building 1930s remains in many places, often now adapted to the tourist trade. A walk along the streets of East Looe, the North Quay at Padstow or the harbour at Mevagissey can bring shudders; well-to-do villas still intrude upon the landscape at Trebetherick (where ironically Sir John Betjeman is laid to rest in St Enodoc churchyard), and the half-decaying clutter of bungalows and holiday shacks along the cliffs at Whitesand Bay shows little sign of being improved or pulled down. The latter are a warning to us of what may happen in the future, at the hundreds of chalet and caravan parks up and down Cornwall, if the financial prosperity sought by their owners and investors does not materialize. After such a procession of past glories, it is a sombre reflection on which to finish this brief survey of Cornish homes and dwellings.

10 Towards the 21st Century

Cornwall approaches the end of this century amid ever-changing patterns and currents. A look back at her history will confirm the view that new influxes, whether of people or ideas, always present fresh dangers but also new possibilities.

During the 1980s tourism has not been the bonanza it was previously, and it is at present a very mixed blessing, with several new patterns developing. The continuing high cost of maintaining hotels will, it seems, confirm the present strong trend towards self-catering holidays. More could certainly be done to utilize those long lines of mausoleums at Bude, Newquay, Falmouth and Penzance during the winter months but so far hotel firms in general have not appeared anxious to extend into the fields of conferences, festivals and seminars. The success of the Pan-Celtic Lowender Perran Festival at Perranporth in October of each year, bringing participants and spectators from all over Britain as well as from the various Celtic countries, is a glowing example of what can be achieved, and the festival receives very little indeed in the way of subsidy or sponsorship. Historic tours of Cornwall, presenting and exploring the Cornish heritage, are another idea which could well be profitable, attracting Cornish exiles from America, Australia and southern Africa as well as the UK.

Cornwall's high proportion of retired and elderly people is already placing considerable strain on the health services; a sign of the times is the dramatic increase in the number of private nursing homes. Among the most neglected sections of the populace are the disabled, for whom much more could and surely should be done: many of them are experienced, mature and intelligent people who could make a significant contribution to the life around them if they were helped to become more mobile. Some are now being trained to use computers at home and thus provide services for business and industry.

Cornwall has always been a land of self-employed people, and this independent trait will of necessity become emphasized as we move towards a society with permanently high unemployment and a need for more leisure services. Craftsmen, fishermen and growers are

Godrevy Lighthouse and Point

combining into co-operatives to help each other market their products. CoSIRA and other bodies attempt, with limited success, to help new business ventures. There is much desirable and necessary social work to be done among the old, the sick and disabled and to help school-leavers find a career or role in life. Much greater effort, encouraged by government and local authorities, could be put into utilizing these wasting resources – people. Many leisure activities themselves can be fruitful and lead to new concepts and ideas; a far greater range of adult educational facilities seems to be not just desirable but essential.

Environmental issues receive a great deal of attention in Cornwall today, as of course they ought to. The re-development of towns and villages and the countryside itself often causes heated campaigns against what is considered undesirable; for instance, unnecessary road improvements, housing estates which do not answer any pressing local need, and cafés and amusements which alter the traditional character of fishing ports. There is often a clash between supporters of what holds promise of more work, such as new mining ventures, and those who wish to see the countryside protected. The threat to Cornish moorlands and their archaeological heritage continues. Recently a number of Iron Age rounds and Bronze Age stone circles were dug up by persons encouraged by a well-known chocolate-maker to seek a golden egg, said to be hidden near an ancient monument: an indefensible campaign of advertising which must never be repeated. The EEC bounty to hill farmers, encouraging them to break in and cultivate moorland, should surely be varied so that strict approval must be obtained, to depend on whether or not the land is valuable archaeologically or as a nature reserve. An irreplaceable Iron Age field system adjacent to Chysauster was recently arbitrarily destroyed by a farmer before planners could be persuaded to protect it.

At least one new activity on our moorlands appears, for the present at least, to pose little danger to the environment. Cornwall's granite rock outcrops are the background and essential feature of an imaginative project being run by the Camborne School of Mines and funded by the EEC and UK Department of Energy: the Geothermal Energy, or 'Hot Rocks', scheme. Huge drilling rigs have been set up in the Rosemanowes quarry near Stithians, with the intention of drilling boreholes into the deep granite, eventually to a depth of six thousand metres. Into these twin shafts water will be forced, to surface again at temperatures of around 180°C; this will be used to generate electricity. The project attracts many visitors from all over the world; it is one of two major schemes of its kind, the other being in New Mexico, USA. It began as long ago as 1973, and grants of £10 million, in 1980, and £11 million, in 1983, have so far been received. Only this type of fractured granite rock, extending to such depth and to temperatures of 230°C, is suitable. One day, perhaps, geothermal

Blackpool China Clay Drying Plant

energy will be used as commonly as North Sea gas or nuclear fission fuel. A question for the future will be: where will the power stations utilizing such energy be sited?

The Cornish Heritage Trust (launched in 1985) is designed to save some of the fast-disappearing legacies of the past which would not be supported by other means. It intends to raise money to buy and refurbish historic buildings and acquire for public use scenic land and objects of art and antiquity which ought to remain in Cornwall. The Trust, with an impressive list of patrons, has bought Castle-an-Dinas near St Columb. It deserves the support of all who wish to protect such things against the tide of development; already Land's End and Lamorna Cove have been sold, no organization or body rich enough being interested in saving them for posterity in their unspoiled state.

Transport matters, as ever, are of the greatest importance to Cornwall. The great emphasis on tourism in recent years has produced improvements to the Cornish road system which were hardly dreamed of twenty years ago – for, of course, they would not be needed if the annual influx had not occurred, with increases every year until 1980. The main A30 road (in the past described as the longest cart-track in the UK) is still woefully inadequate on many of its stretches: heavy transports still thunder through the villages of Blackwater, Zelah, Mitchell, Summercourt and Fraddon, which by any law of priority should surely all have been bypassed a decade ago. Yet there is a seven-mile dual carriageway bypass around Camborne-Redruth, now extended a further eight miles to beyond Hayle, bringing the westward traveller to within sight of Penzance; another immense dual road curves through woodland and heath to circumvent Bodmin; a third sweeps past Launceston into Devon, and a fourth speeds traffic past Liskeard towards Plymouth. Other ancient Cornish roads are gradually being straightened and widened to allow tourists and residents to drive from one town to another a few minutes more quickly than they otherwise would have been able to. No one wants bottlenecks, and nothing is more frustrating than to sit in a queue of lorries, coaches and cars, all fuming and polluting the countryside, but perhaps we in Cornwall are now in danger of worshipping that notorious twentieth-century deity, speed, and the delightfully rambling and inconsequential nature of some of our by-roads is now threatened.

Air transport is gradually becoming more essential: a local airways firm operates services from St Mawgan to London and the Isles of Scilly; British Airways helicopters fly daily to and from the Isles of Scilly; Plymouth and Exeter airports link Cornwall with Brittany, the Channel Isles and Ireland. Brittany Ferries, sailing their large car carrying ships from Roscoff to Plymouth, offer an easy and relatively inexpensive means of reaching the Continent; they are reviving the traditional links between Cornwall and Brittany with a growing two-way traffic. Coastal shipping is still at a low ebb, but china clay ships work regularly from Par and Fowey, and oil tankers come to discharge at Falmouth – where the container port proposal is still under discussion, planning and canvassing. It would seem simple good sense to develop this great harbour again as the first in Britain, but other large ports are competing for the prize, and at the time of writing the issue is still in doubt.

Cornwall still has no university. The nearest is Exeter, which does

Early warning system: Cleeve Camp, Morwenstow

provide, at Redruth, the Institute of Cornish Studies under its own resident Cornish Director. At graduate level the Institute studies and reports on activities as varied as the Cornish dialect, place-names, geological features, farming patterns, marine biology, industrial developments and the racial characteristics of the Cornish themselves. Its highly technical reports may seem mystifying to many, but public seminars are being held to publicize this work, which one guesses will turn out to be of immense value in the future.

The towns and villages of Cornwall are witnessing the gradual creation of new communities, as newcomers move in, buy and renovate old buildings and enter parish life. They come for a less hectic and complicated life, governed by the placid rhythms of the seasons: many of them are deliberately seeking an alternative to city or suburban life and take the trouble to learn about Cornwall, its

Goonhilly Earth Satellite Station

history and traditions; some learn the Cornish language. Such people have a great deal to contribute to the future. The Cornish themselves, the aboriginal Celts or pre-Celts, continue to till the soil, to fish and ply their age-old trades, but they feel inarticulately that they are still overlooked and underprivileged, as the seasonal invasions of tourists arrives and more and more 'foreigners' take over the places they know. Some still survive and even prosper in business. But numbers of Cornishmen and women who have gone far across the world to make careers for themselves are now coming home to retire, still vigorous and active, and throw themselves into working for Cornwall. They join and run societies, political and cultural, and they too learn Kernewek and often become Bards of Gorseth Kernow for their services. They prod the five Westminster MPs (only two of them Cornish) to action, and remind the MEP who represents both Cornwall and Plymouth under present arrangements, that he forgets the land beyond the Tamar at his peril.

But over and beyond these matters looms the question that will eventually decide whether indeed there is to be a future for Cornwall – or even for Britain and Europe. Our present commitment to nuclear power and defence places Cornwall in the forefront of any possible holocaust: the steel fences of the Combined Services Operation Station at Morwenstow protect the great white saucers receiving messages from outer space; the massive barriers of RAF St Mawgan and RNAS Culdrose hint plainly at what is being stockpiled behind them. In 1980–81 protests against the possibility of a nuclear power station being erected in Luxulyan parish resulted in the Central Electricity Generating Board opting for a site elsewhere. Was that battle fought in vain – is all we value, all we have inherited from that marvellous and manifold Cornish past, increasingly at risk – forever to be subject to the paranoias and power politics of the super-powers?

Some of us protest, hold vigils and marches; others are bewildered and undecided; some see the nuclear umbrella, despite its horrific implications, as the only hope of maintaining the precarious peace we have become accustomed to. As so often during the past, our land is under threat, this time in a way unparallelled in history. New answers are needed; only the people of Cornwall and Britain, given the time and a united desire, can provide them.

Select Bibliography

Bachin W. G. V., *Cornwall: An Illustrated Essay on the History of the Landscape* (London, 1954)

Betjeman, J., *The Shell Guide to Cornwall* (London, 1964)

Bottrell, W., *Traditions and Hearthside Stories of West Cornwall* (two volumes) (Penzance, 1870, 1873)

Bottrell, W., *Stories and Folk-lore of West Cornwall* (Penzance, 1880)

Brown, H. Miles, *The Church in Cornwall* (Truro, 1964)

Carew, Richard (ed. F. E. Halliday), *The Survey of Cornwall* (New York, 1969)

Chesher, F. M. & V., *The Cornishman's House* (Truro, 1968)

Coate, M., *Cornwall in the Great Civil War and Interregnum, 1642–1660* (Oxford, 1933)

Collins, Wilkie, *Rambles Beyond Railways* (London, 1851)

Journals of the Cornwall Archaeological Society, *Cornish Archaeology* (Hayle, Exeter, 1968–83)

Elliott-Binns, L. E., *Medieval Cornwall* (London, 1955)

Ellis, P. Berresford, *The Cornish Language and its Literature* (London, 1974)

Halliday, F. E., *History of Cornwall* (London, 1975)

Henderson, Charles, *Essays in Cornish History* (Oxford, 1935)

Henderson, Charles, *Old Cornish Bridges and Streams* (Truro, 1972)

Hunt, Robert, *Popular Romances of the West* (London, 1881)

Jenkin, A. K. H., *Cornwall and its People* (Newton Abbot, 1970)

Jenner, Henry, *A Handbook of the Cornish Language* (London, 1904)

Keast, J., *'The King of Mid-Cornwall' – The Life of Joseph Thomas Treffry (1782–1850)* (Redruth, 1982)

Norden, John, *A Topographical and Historical Survey of Cornwall* (Newcastle upon Tyne, 1966)

Pearce, S. M., *The Kingdom of Dumnonia: Studies in History and Tradition in South Western Britain AD 350–1150* (Padstow, 1978)

Pearse, Richard, *The Ports and Harbours of Cornwall* (St Austell, 1964)

Penderill-Church, J., *William Cookworthy 1705–1780* (Truro, 1972)

Pevsner, Sir Nikolaus, *The Buildings of England: Cornwall* (Harmondsworth, 1970)

Proctor, Ida, *Visitors to Cornwall* (Redruth, 1982)

Rowe, John, *Cornwall in the Industrial Revolution* (Liverpool, 1952)

Rowse, A. L., *Tudor Cornwall: Portrait of Society* (London, 1941)

Sheppard, P., *The Historic Towns of Cornwall: An Archaeological Survey* (Truro, 1980)
Tregellas, W. H., *Tourist's Guide to Cornwall and the Scilly Isles* (London, 1880)
Weatherhill, Craig, *Bellerion: Ancient Sites of Land's End* (Penzance, 1981)
Weatherhill, Craig, *Cornubia* (Penzance, 1985)
Whetter, J. C., *Cornwall in the 17th Century: an Economic History of Kernow* (Padstow, 1974)

Index

Abbey House, Padstow, 197, 198
Acton Castle, 190
'Allan Apple', St Just, 130
Allen, A., 197
Allen, River, 58
Almshouses, 177–9
Altarnun, 137, 147
  stone circles, 22
Amalveor Hoard, 26
Angel Hotel, Helston, 199
Angrouse, 181
Antony House, 190
Ardevora Veor, 51
Arthur, Pendragon, 133
Arundell family, 143, 144, 185
Arundell, Sir John, 185
Arwennack House, 185
Athelstan, King, 99, 136
Augustine, St, 136
'Australia's Little Cornwall', 159

Baldhu, 149
Ballantyne, R. M., 158–9
Bant's Carn, Scillies, 19
Baptists, 146, 153
Barrows, 121
Basset family, 192
Basset, Sir Francis, 167 *see also* de Dunstanville
Beaker People, 21
Beersheba Stone, 22
Bennetto, W. M. (Bard Abransek), 129
Béroul, 49
Betjeman, Sir John, 65, 203
Black Death, 67, 139
Blight, J. T., 105
Blind Fiddler, 22, 23
Blisland, 58, 59
Bochym Manor, 189
Boconnoc House, 48, 190, 191
Bodenor, William, 127
Bodinnick, 49
Bodmin, 62, 65–7, 115, 173
  Moor, 17, 19, 20, 23, 24, 55, 164, 166, 176, 179
  relics of St Petroc, 41
  Riding, 122
Bodmin-Wadebridge Railway, 68
Bodwen, rapier mould, 26
Boleigh Fogou, 30, 32
Borlase, Dr William, 22, 23, 36, 146
Boscastle, 79–80, 103, 106, 165, 180
Boscaswell, Lower, Fogou, 30
Boscawen Un stone circle, 22
Bosence, Hayle, 31, 41, 56
Boskednan stone circle, 22
Bosporthennis courtyard houses, 30
  Fogou, 30
Bossiney, 103
Bosullow, courtyard houses, 30
  Fogou, 30
Boswarva, Madron, 30
Boswen longstone, 22
Bottrell, William, 130, 182
Botus Fleming, 43
Boyton, 39
Bray, Billy, 147–8, 152
Breage Church, 141
Broad, Thomas, 131
Broccoli, 168
Bronscombe, Bishop Walter, 138
Bronze Age, 21–7
Brown Willy, 46
Brunel, I. K., Tamar Bridge, 42
Bryan, William, 147
Bude, 79, 105, 110, 111, 173
  Canal, 38, 80
Burnard, Neville N., 72–3

Cadsonbury, 44
Caer Bran, 35
Caerhayes Castle, 193–4

Calenick, 193
Callington, 33, 63–4, 103
Calstock, 42, 101
  Viaduct, 169
Camborne, 74–5, 148, 173, 176
Camel estuary, Hawker's Cove, 61
Camel, River, 17, 57, 61
Camelford, 57, 58, 67, 115, 167
Canals:
  Bude–Holsworthy, 79, 105
  Moorswater–Looe, 96
Caradon mines, 159
  quarries, 96, 162
Carclew, 192
Carew, Richard, 117, 127, 162, 168, 169, 175, 190
Carfury longstone, 22
Cargreen, 43
Carn Brea, 20–1
  Castle, 101
Carn Euny Fogou, 30
  Iron Age Village, 30
Carn Kenidjack, holed stones, 24, 26
Carnon, River, 52
Carnsew quarries, 162
Carrick Roads, 53, 54
Cassiterides, the Tin Isles, 154
Castilly Henge, 21
Castle an Dinas, St Columb, 28, 161
  West Penwith, 162
Castle Dore, 33
Castle Horneck, 190
Castle Killibury, 33
Castlewich, 21
Cataclewse quarries and stone, 162, 175
Celtic deities, 132
  festivals, 132
Celts, 27–31, 165–6
Chantries, 68, 141
Charlestown, 92, 93, 164
Cheesewring, The, 102
  quarries, 44
Chesher, F. J. & V. M., 179
China Clay industry, 162–4, 207
Chough, Cornish, 103
Christmas carols, 131
  customs, 130–1
Chysauster, 29, 30
Clemo, Jack, 51
Clowance, 54, 193
Cober, River, 53
Collamere (St Faith's), 197
Colleges of canons:
  Crantock, 138, 140
  St Buryan, 138
  St Endellion, 138
  St Germans, 138
Collins, Wilkie, 103–4
Come-to-Good, Quaker meeting house, 146, 153
Connor, Manor and Downs, 56
Constantine Fogou, 30
  'Island', 17
  Maen Pern stone, 23
  Prince, 135
  the Tolven stone, 26
Cookworthy, William, 69, 162–3
Copper mining, 157–9
Cornish language, 125–30
  Unit houses, 203
Cornwall Archaeological Society, 24, 36
  Committee for Rescue Archaeology, 24
Coryton, Sir William, 190
Cotehele House, 175, 183–4, 184
  Quay, 43
Couch, T. Q., 122, 130
Courtnay, M. A., 130
Courtyard houses, 29–30
Crag, the, Maenporth, 197
Craik, Mrs, 105
Cranken, courtyard houses, 30
Crantock, 57, 147
Creation plays, 127
Crofto, courtyard houses, 30
Crosses:
  Celtic, 135
  Cornish, 36
'Crying the Neck', 122, 124–5

Damelioc Fort, 51
Davy, Sir Humphrey, 77
Daymer House, 197
de Dunstanville, Lord, 72
de Lank, River, 58
Defoe, Daniel, 100
Delabole, 106, 116, 162
Devil's Quoit, St Columb, 19
Dibden, Charles, 200
Diodorus Siculus, 154
Dissenters, 144–9
Dockacre House, Launceston, 199
Doniert Stone, 35
Drift longstones, 22

Duloe stone circle, 22
Dunmere, 58

Eagle Hotel, Launceston, 201
Ebbingford Manor, 191
Edgcumbe Hotel, Newquay, 201
Edgcumbe, Sir Piers, 42, 184
Sir Richard, 182, 184
Edward VI, King, 141
Edwards, John, 84
Egbert, King, 136
Eliot, Sir John, 193
Elizabeth, Queen, 143
Entrance graves, 18, 19
Erth Barton, 185
Ethy House, 190
Eusticke, 'Mad' Squire, 147

Fal, River, 50–3
Falmouth, 89–91, 100, 101, 107, 172, 173, 199
Farming, 165–9
Fernacre stone circle, 22
Fiennes, Celia, 99–100
Fishing, 169–72
Fogous, 30–1
Fowey, 93–4, 95, 99, 101, 170, 178
estuary, 108–9
museum, 115
rapier, 26
River, 46–9
Fox, George, 145
Friends, Society of (Quakers), 144–5, 153

Gannel, River, 57, 83
Geoffrey of Monmouth, 33
Gillan, 53
Glasney College, Penryn, 91, 127, 138
Glebe House, Philleigh, 191
Glynn House, 193
Godolphin family, 199
House, 189–90
Godolphin, Sidney, 190
Godrevy Lighthouse, 205
Golitha Falls, 46, 47
Goonhilly Downs, 17
Earth Satellite Station, 210
Gorseth Kernow, 125, 126
Goss Moor, 50
Grade Church, 139
Grahame, Kenneth, 49
Great Rebuild, the, 179–81
Great Western Hotel, Newquay, 111, 201
Grenville, Sir John, 144
Sir Richard, 43, 80
Greystone Bridge, 41
Grose, Samuel, 157
Gunnislake, 42
Gurnard's Head, 105
Gweek, 54
Gwennap Pit, 147
Wesley Memorial Chapel, 150
Gwithian, 27
Gwryans an Bys (The Creation of the World), 127

Haliggey Fogou, 30
Hallowe'en, 130
Harlyn Bay, Iron Age graves, 31
House, 182, 185
lunulae, 26
Harvey, John (foundry), 84
Harvey's packet, 168
Hawker, Revd Robert Stephen, 38, 147, 149, 181, 182
Hayle, 84, 103, 174
estuary, 56
Headland Hotel, Newquay, 201
Helford River, 53
Heligan, 187
Helston, 54, 75–7, 78, 166, 173, 199
Furry Dance, 119, 121
Henderson, Charles, 40
Henry II, King, 139
Henry VII, King, 155
Henry VIII, King, 53, 141
Hensbarrow tumuli, 24
Hermits, medieval, 141
Herodsfoot, 45
Herring driving, 171–2
Hill forts, 28–9
Hingston Down, battle of, 136
quarry, 162
Holed stones, 24, 26
Holmbush tumuli, 24
Holy wells, 135–6
Horsebridge, 40, 41
Hotels and inns, 201
Howell (Hywal), King, 36
Hunt, Robert, 130, 183
Hurlers, the, stone circle, 22, 25
Hurling, 117–19
at St Columb, 118

Ictis, 154, 196
Illogan, 176
Ince Castle, 187
Indulgences, 41
Inney, River, 41
Iseult, 35, 52

Jenner, Henry, 125, 129
John, King, 155

Keigwin House, Mousehole, 197
Kelliwic, 33
Kenstec, Celtic abbot-bishop, 136
Kilbirnie Hotel, Newquay, 201
Kilkhampton, 38, 166
Killiowe, 193
King Arthur's Castle Hotel, Tintagel, 201
King Harry Passage, 51
Kingston, Sir Anthony, 142

Lanherne, 186
Lanhydrock House, 48, 187, 188
Lanlivery, rapier mould, 26
Lanooe, St Kew, 181
Lanteglos Cross, Camelford, 133
Lantyan, 33
Lanyon, 179
  Quoit, 19
Launceston, 39, 41, 62–3, 100, 103, 141, 173, 174, 199, 200
Lawhitton, 41
Leaze Circle, 22
Leland, John, 99
Lelant, 56
  Beersheba Stone, 22
  churchyard, Celtic Cross, 134
Lemon family, 192–3
Lerryn, 48–9
Lhuyd, Edward, 129
Lifeboat, Padstow, 112
Lifeboat station, Sennen, 171
Linkinhorne, 141
Liskeard, 64, 101, 174, 197, 199
Lizard, The, 89, 176
Loam, Michael, 159
Loe Pool and Bar, 54
Longstones, 21–2
  inscribed, 35
Looe, 44, 45–6, 96, 100, 101, 110, 172
Looe–Caradon Railway, 64, 96
Looe Union Canal, 44
Lostwithiel, 48, 49, 64–5, 142
Louden Hill stone circle, 22
Lovering, John, 164
Lunulae, 26
Luxulyan quarries, 93, 162
  River, 49
Lynher, River, 44

Maclean, Sir John, 36
Madron, Carfury longstone, 22
  courtyard houses, 30
  holy well, 136
Maen Pern, 23
Malory, Sir Thomas, 33
Manorial system, 166
Manumissions, Bodmin, 137
Marazion, 41, 77, 89
Marhays, 189
Mark, King, 33, 41, 52
Marlborough House, Falmouth, 199
Mary Tudor, Queen, 142–3
Maton, Dr. W. G., 101, 102, 103
Mawgan Porth, Dark Age settlement, 179
Mayne, St Cuthbert, 143–4
Men Scryfa, 35
Men an Tol, 24
Menabilly, 190
Menhirs, 21, 22, 23
Merritt, Thomas, 131
Merry Maidens, Rosmodress, 22
Mesolithic (Middle Stone) Age, 17
Mesolithic forests:
  Bar Pool, 18
  Falmouth, 18
  Gillan, 18
  Hayle, 18
  Little Petherick, 18
  Luxulyan, 18
  Maenporth, 18
  Maer Lake, 18
  Marazion, 18
  Perranporth, 18
  Portmellon, 18
Methodism, 146–9
Metropole Hotel, Padstow, 201
Mevagissey, 92, 110, 164, 165, 172, 203
Midsummer bonfires, 120, 121
Mills, 168
Minack Theatre, 114, 115
Mines and mining:
  Bosigran Engine House, 156

Botallack, 100, 104, 111, 159
Caradon district, 159
Carclaze, 69, 164
Carharrack, 157
Carn Brea Complex, 74
Carnkie, 74
Carnmenellis District, 159
Castle an Dinas, 161
Cligga Head, 161
Cook's Kitchen, 74, 102, 157
Dolcoath, 74, 102, 157
Geevor, 116, 161
Godolphin Bal, 77
Levant, 111, 159, 160
Mount Wellington, 161
Pednandrea, 75
South Crofty, 74, 165
St Ives Consols, 111
techniques, 156–9
tin miners underground, 160
Tresavean, 159
Trevenson, 74
Wheal Coates, 158
Wheal Concord, 161
Wheal Jane, 161
Wheal Pendarves, 74, 161
Wherry, 101
Moditonham House, 190
Molesworth Arms, the, Wadebridge, 200, 201
Molesworth, Sir William, 192
Monasteries:
Bodmin, 138, 140
Celtic, 136, 138
Launceston, 138, 140
medieval, 137–8
Minster, 139
St Michael's Mount, 137–8, 196
Truro, 138
Mordred, 33
Morvah, courtyard houses, 30
Morval House, 187
Morwellham Quay, 43
Morwenstow, 106, 139, 181, 183, 209
Mousehole, 56, 77, 86, 87, 172, 197
Mudgeon, 181
Mulfra Quoit, 20
Vean, 30
Mullion Cove, 89
Mummers' plays, 130
Murray's Handbook, 105
Mylor Church, 138

Nance, R. Morton, 129, 130
Nash, John, 194
Nash, John, RA, 199
Neolithic Age, 19–21
Newbridge, Gunnislake (Tamar), 42
Newbridge, Lynher, 44, 45
Newcomen engines, 69, 157
Newlyn, 87, 88, 172
Newquay, 82–4, 85, 106, 107, 110, 111, 201
Newton Ferrers, 190
Nicholas, Stephen, 131
Nine Maidens, derivation of name, 22
St Breock, 22
Noall, R. J., 24
Norman churches, 139, 140
Norris, Edwin, 129
North Petherwin, 39
Notter Bridge, 44

Ogam script, 35
Ogbeare Hall, 180, 181
Old Cornwall Societies, 14, 36, 121
Old Custom House Inn, Padstow, 201
Old Mill, Treknow, 201
Old Rectory, St Columb, 68, 197
Ordinalia plays, 91, 126–7, 128
Ottery, River, 40
Oyster fisheries, 170

Padstow, 81–2, 83, 100, 106, 110, 111, 112, 115, 172, 173, 197, 198, 201, 202
Crugmeer (the Great Barrow), 24
stone cottages, 178
Obby Oss and May Day, 119, 120
Padstow-Wadebridge Railway, 60
Palmer's Bridge, 41, 46
Par, 49–50, 92–3, 178
Passion and Resurrection plays, 127
Paul, 127, 178
Pawton Manor, 136
Quoit, 19
Pelmear, Kenneth, 131
Pelynt sword, 26
Pencarrow House, 101, 191
Pendarves Quoit, 19
Pendeen, 149
Boswen Longstone, 22
Vau Fogou, 30
Pendennis Castle, 53, 185
Pengenna, 179

Pengersick Castle, 182
Penheale, 187–9
Penrice, 193
Penrose House, 54, 189
Penryn, 41, 91, 173, 199
Pentewan, 69
quarries, 162
Pentire Point, 17, 61
Pentreath, Dolly, 127
Penventon Hotel, Redruth, 201
Penzance, 77–8, 87, 99, 100, 101, 110, 172, 199, 201
Perceuil, River, 53
Perranarworthal, 52
Perranporth, 107, 110, 111, 112
Perran Wharf, 52
Perranuthnoe, 114
Pentillie Castle, 43, 193
Peter, Thurstan, 20, 130
Pevsner, Sir Nikolaus, 195
Phillack, 56
Philleigh, Glebe House, 191
Phillpotts, Bishop Henry, 149
Piggot, Prof. Stuart, 26
Piran Round, 104, 110
Place, St Anthony in Roseland, 195–6
Place House, Fowey, 196
Pococke, Dr Richard, 100–1
Polcarne House, 197
Polperro, 94–6, 97
Polston (Polson) Bridge, 40
Polyphant, 162
Pont Creek, 49
Port Eliot, 193
Porthcallum, 55
Porthleven, 89, 172, 173
Porthmeor, courtyard houses, 30
Fogou, 30
Port Isaac, 80–1, 111, 112
Portreath, 84
Portwrinkle, 96, 171, 201
Poughill, 79, 141
Poundstock, 139, 142
Prayer Book Rebellion, 127, 141–2
Praze-an-Beeble, 176
Pre-emption of tin, 155
Prideaux House, Luxulyan, 186
Place, Padstow, 183, 186
Probus Church, 141

Quakers, 144–5, 153
Quarrying, 162
Quiller-Couch, Sir Arthur ('Q'), 49
Quoits, 19

Rashleigh, Charles, 92
Rawe, Richard, 144
Rebellion of 1497, 155
Red Lion Hotel, St Columb, 122, 201
Red River, 56–7
Redruth, 75, 76, 101, 116, 176, 201
Relubbus, 55
Repton, Sir Humphrey, 193
Respryn Bridge, 48
Restormel Castle, 47
House, 194
Restronguet Creek, 52
Rialobranus, 35
Rialton House, 185
Ricatus, King, 35
Riots, 167
Roberts, Sir Richard (Lord Robartes), 48, 187
Robinson, P. F., 193
Roche Rock, 101, 140, 141
Rock village and quay, 60–1
Roman Catholics, 136–44, 152–3
Roman coin hoards, 33
milestones, 31
mining, 155
possible roads, 31
Roscarrack, 181
Roscarrock, Nicholas, 139, 144
Rosecadghill, 181, 190
Roskruge Barton, 181
Rosmeryn, 181
Royal Cornwall Polytechnic Society, Falmouth, 107, 145
Royal Hotel, Truro, 201
Royal Institution of Cornwall, Truro, 72
Ruan Lanihorne, 51

St Agnes, 177
St Anthony in Roseland, 139, 195
St Aubyn family, 193, 196
St Aubyn, J. P., 149, 196, 197
St Austell, 68–9, 72, 99, 100, 116, 141, 174, 199
River, 50
St Breaca, 134
St Breock, Men Gortos Stone, 22
St Breward stone circle, 22
St Brioc, 134–5

St Buryan, 99
Cross, 135
Pridden longstone, 22
Trelew longstone, 22
St Cadoc, 134
St Cleer, 136
Craddock Moor stone circle, 22
Doniert Stone, 35
St Clement, 176
St Clether, 136
St Columb Major, 68, 117–19, 122, 201
St Crantoc, 57, 134, 136
St David, 135
St Day, 149
St Docco, 181
St Endellion, inscribed stone, 35
Music Festival, 114
St Erth, 55, 56
St Fingar (Gwinear), 134
St Germans, 114, 139, 178, 193
River, 44
St Hilary, 139
Fogou, 30
St Hydroc, 187
St Ia, 134
St Ives, 84–6, 88, 102, 107, 110, 111, 113, 115, 147, 165, 170, 171, 172, 173, 194, 201
St Juliot, lunula, 26
St Just in Penwith, 101, 147
in Roseland, 143
St Keverne, 176, 177
sword-blade, 26
St Kew, inscribed stone, 35
St Mary's (Scilly), 115
St Mawes, 92, 113
Castle, 53
St Merryn Church, 145
St Michael's Mount, 18, 41, 89, 154, 192, 196
St Neot, 47
St Nonna, 135
St Patrick, 134
St Petroc, 65, 66, 67, 81, 135, 139
St Piran, 136
St Piran's Cross, 36
relics, 139
St Samson, 134, 135
St Stephen's by Launceston, 62–3
St Stephen-in-Brannell, 162
St Thomas Church, Launceston, 39, 63
St Veep, 142
Trevollard House, 182
Saints, Celtic, 134–6
Saltash, 43–4, 97–8, 173
Samhain, 130
Sancreed, 135
Saxon strip farming, 166
Scilly, Isles of, 19, 112, 168, 169
Sconner House, 193
Sea Mills, 60
Sedding, J., 149
Seining, 170–1
Selus Stone, 35
Sennen, 171
Shaw, Revd S. S., 101
Shillingham House, 190
Slaughterbridge, 33
Sloane, Sir John, 193
Smeaton, John, 84, 92
Smugglers, 149
Spry, Admiral Thomas, 196
Stafford, Bishop, 139
Stanbury, 185
Stannary Charters, 155
Stannary Parliament (Cornish Convocation), 155
Stannon Stones, 22
Stapledon, Bishop Walter, 139
Stepper Point, 17, 61, 82
Stokes, Whitley, 129
Stow Barton, 189
Street, G. E., 149, 196–7
Stripple Stones, 21
Stuart House, Liskeard, 197

Tamar, River, 38–44
Tamarstone, 38
Tehidy House, 192
Temple, 41
Tewdr (Theodore), Prince of Meneage, 134
Thorough Guide to North Devon and North Cornwall, 110
Ti Du ('black house'), 179
Tin coining, 101, 155–6
Tintagel, 103, 106, 111, 136, 139, 173, 180, 201
Tintagel, inscribed stones, 35
Tolven, the, 26
Tonacombe manor house, 185
Torpoint, 96–7
Towednack, Amalveor Hoard, 26
Trebetherick, 203

Trebyan Quoit, 19
Trecarrel Manor, 185
Trecarrel, Sir Henry, 141, 185, 197, 199
Treen Common stone circle, 22
Treffry, J. T., 50, 92, 196
 Viaduct, 50, 196
Treforda, 179
Tregarden, 189
Tregaseal stone circle, 22
Tregear Fort, Nanstallon, 31, 41, 58
Tregellas, W. H., 110
Tregenna Castle, St Ives, 194, 201
Tregian, Francis, 144
Tregirls, 181
Treglos Hotel, Constantine Bay, 113
Tregony, 51, 178
Tregothnan House, 194, 195
Trelan Bahow, 31
Trelawne House, 187
Trelawny ballad, the, 38
Trelawny, Sir Harry, 152
 Sir Jonathan, 187
Trelissick House, 52, 193, 194
Trelowarren, 189
Trematon Castle, 193
Trenethick Barton, 181
Trengoffe, 181
Trengrouse, Henry, 77
Trenowth, 197
Trereiffe, 190
Trerice House, 185, 186
Tresungers, 181
Tresvenneck Drift longstone, 22
Trethevy Quoit, 19, 34
Trevail, Sylvanus, 201
Trevanion, Charles of Caerhayes, 51
 Charles of Cregoe, 51
Trevean Round, Morvah, 30
 Fogou, 30
Trevear, St Stephen, 181
Treverbyn Bridge, 47
Trevisker, 27
Trevithick, Richard, 156, 167
Trevollard, St Veep, 181, 182
Trevone, Iron Age cemetery, 31
Trevose Head, 18
Trewen Hall, 189
Trewithen House, 190
Trewitten, 179
Treworgey, 190
Trippet Stones, 22
Tristan, 33, 35, 52
Troon, 177
Truro, 70–1, 72–4, 100, 101, 114, 173, 200, 201, 202
 Cathedral, 73, 149, 152
Try longstone, 22
Twowatersfoot, 47
Tywardreath, 49

Ulcagnus, 35
Uther, 33

Veryan, round houses, 176
Vulliamy, Lewis, 194
Vyvyan family, 189

Wadebridge, 68, 167, 173, 200, 201
 Bridge, 59–60, 69
Wallysborough, Sir Roger, 139
Ward Lock's Guide, 112
Waterburst, of 1847, 58
Waterhouse, Alfred, 197
Watt, James, 157
Webb's Hotel, Liskeard, 199
Wedgwood, Josiah, 163
Welltown, 181
Wendron, 116
 stone circles, 22
Werrington, 39
Wesley, John, 56, 146–7
Wesleyan movement, 147
Wessex culture, 26
Wheal Martyn China Clay Museum, 115
White, Walter, 80, 105
Whitefield, George, 147
White Hart Hotel, St Austell, 199
White Hart Inn, Launceston, 199
Whitesand Bay, 203
Wilkins, William, 194
Williams, Revd R., 129
Woolf, Arthur, 157
Worthyvale, inscribed stone, 35, 58
Wrecking, 149
Wrecks:
 Bencoolen, 79
 Elizabeth Scown, 79
 on Doom Bar, Padstow, 82
Wrestling, Cornish, 122, 123
Wrotham, William de, 155

Zennor, Kerrow longstone, 22
 Treen Common stone circle, 22